ABIDE IN THE HEART OF

CHRIST

ABIDE IN THE HEART OF

CHRIST

A 10-DAY PERSONAL RETREAT WITH ST. IGNATIUS LOYOLA

Joe Laramie, S.J.

Based on the *Spiritual Exercises*

Ave Maria Press   AVE   Notre Dame, Indiana

Imprimi Potest
Very Reverend Ronald A. Mercier, Provincial
USA Central and Southern Province of the Society of Jesus

Founded in 1865, Ave Maria Press is a ministry of the United States Province of Holy Cross.

www.avemariapress.com

Paperback: ISBN-13 978-1-59471-891-5

E-book: ISBN-13 978-1-59471-892-2

Cover image of St. Ignatius of Loyola ©Julie Lonneman, courtesy of Trinity Stores, www.trinitystores.com, 800-699-4482.

Cover background © gettyimages.com.

Cover and text design by Katherine J. Ross.

Printed and bound in the United States of America.

Library of Congress Cataloging-in-Publication Data
Names: Laramie, Joe, author.
Title: Abide in the heart of Christ : a 10-day personal retreat with St. Ignatius Loyola based on the spiritual exercises / Joe Laramie, S.J.
Description: Notre Dame, IN : Ave Maria Press, 2019. | Includes bibliographical references.
Identifiers: LCCN 2019016253 | ISBN 9781594718915 (pbk.)
Subjects: LCSH: Ignatius, of Loyola, Saint, 1491-1556. Exercitia spiritualia. | Spirituality--Catholic Church. | Spiritual exercises. | Spiritual retreats.
Classification: LCC BX2179.L8 L37 2019 | DDC 248.3--dc23
LC record available at https://lccn.loc.gov/2019016253

Contents

Acknowledgments

Thank you to my family and friends for their encouragement and support throughout this project. Special thanks to my Jesuit brothers, superiors, spiritual directors, and mentors. Our best conversations about St. Ignatius and the spiritual life were usually over morning coffee or evening beer. I appreciate your love, prayers, and suggestions. My Jesuit and Franciscan proofreaders offered invaluable feedback.

I'm also grateful to all the fine teachers who shaped me in my Catholic and Jesuit schools as well as the teachers and colleagues I worked with at Jesuit schools, parishes, and retreat centers. I admire your faithfulness, creativity, and generosity. My current and former students, retreatants, and spiritual directees inspired me by sharing their stories, prayers, joys, and sorrows. If you live or have lived in these places, thank you (you know who you are): Florissant, Missouri; St. Louis, Missouri; St. Paul, Minnesota; Chicago, Illinois; Kansas City, Missouri; Denver, Colorado; Boston, Massachusetts; Bethlehem, Connecticut; Portland, Oregon; and Belize.

Catherine Owers, editor, and the staff at Ave Maria Press were professional, wise, and faithful every step of the way. Theirs is a holy ministry.

I dedicate this book to the Sacred Heart of Jesus and the Immaculate Heart of Mary. Lord Jesus and Mother Mary, you love us very much. Unite our hearts to yours!

Ad majorem Dei gloriam.

A Retreat with the *Spiritual Exercises* of St. Ignatius

Come away by yourselves to a

deserted place and rest a while.

—Mark 6:31

You're busy. I know. And you want to grow in your faith. But who has time to pray? Perhaps when you do pray, you feel distracted. Then the thought occurs to you, "What am I supposed to pray about?" Have I got a book for you! In fact, it's the one that you're holding right now.

WHAT'S THIS BOOK ABOUT?

Abide in the Heart of Christ will help you to grow closer to Christ and to live more fully in his love each day. In this book, you'll use the writings of St. Ignatius of Loyola as a guide to deepen your relationship with Jesus. Ignatius founded the Society of Jesus (more commonly known as the Jesuits) and helped people to deepen their faith in Europe in the 1500s. Ignatius's *Spiritual Exercises* continue to help thousands of people around the globe to grow in their relationship with Christ and live their faith in the world today. *Abide in the Heart of Christ* is based on the *Spiritual Exercises*. Written at an introductory level, this book can help you strengthen your Christian life, no matter your age or experience with retreats. You do not need a theology degree to use it! All you need is a mind, a heart, and a desire to follow Christ more fully.

This book is not primarily focused on delivering information. There are many fine books with great information about Church history, understanding the Old Testament, and so on. However, this book will help in the formation of your heart according to Christ. Over the next several days, we'll embark on a retreat together. We won't be trying to learn a lot of facts here; rather, we'll seek to deepen our relationship with Christ. We will use our minds, of course: to help us know and love Christ more fully. To use an analogy, we won't be learning about geology; we'll be climbing a mountain. We won't be reading about flowers; we'll be growing a garden.

This book is written for Catholics and other Christians, but it can also assist anyone seeking deeper spiritual meaning and purpose in life.

WHAT IS A RETREAT?

A retreat is a time away with God. In the gospels, we see Jesus himself going to the desert for forty days of prayer (Mt 4:1–11). He also invited his disciples to take time for retreat when he said, "Come away by yourselves to a deserted place and rest a while" (Mk 6:31). Throughout the centuries, Christians have taken time for retreat in a variety of ways and locations: going to churches, monasteries, shrines, deserts, or retreat houses. Some retreats occur over a weekend, or over a week. Some people go on retreat in daily life, making special time for prayer amid their commitments to family, work, or school. That's what we'll be doing: making a ten-day retreat in daily life.

WHO WAS ST. IGNATIUS?

Ignatius, born in 1491, was the youngest child of a large, wealthy family in Loyola, Spain. The following year, in 1492, "Columbus sailed the ocean blue" and discovered the American continents. Twenty-five years later, Martin Luther posted his *Ninety-Five Theses* on the doors of a German cathedral, inaugurating the Protestant Reformation. This was an era of profound change and turbulence in the Church and throughout the world.

At age twenty-nine, Ignatius was serving in the Spanish army and fought in a battle against the French in the town of Pamplona, Spain. Swords clanged and shots fired. A cannonball struck Ignatius in the knee, shattering his leg, and he collapsed to the ground in agony. He was carried on a stretcher back to his family's castle, and everyone presumed that he would die. Incredibly, he began a slow recovery. As he lay on his bed, he underwent a powerful spiritual conversion. He read a book about the lives of the saints and a book of reflections on the gospels. He reflected on his own life and saw a prideful, self-centered young man who loved honor and personal glory. Slowly, he was drawn to the idea of devoting his life to the service of Christ and the Church. He regained his health, though he would walk with a limp for the rest of his life. Ignatius left Spain and wandered across Europe, seeking out religious shrines and holy people—asking for their prayers and advice.

He visited the Holy Land and spent time studying at the University of Paris. In Paris, he gathered with other like-minded students for prayer and conversation. Together they preached, served the poor, and led simple retreats. Ignatius was ordained a priest, and in 1540, he founded the Society of Jesus. His roommate in Paris was inspired to join Ignatius in his work. That roommate was Francis Xavier, and he was among the first men to take vows as a Jesuit. (Xavier later traveled to Asia as a heroic Christian missionary, preaching the Gospel in India and Japan. He was canonized in 1622 for his faith and labor.)

Under Ignatius's leadership, the Jesuit order spread rapidly throughout Europe and around the world—establishing schools, missions, churches, and retreat centers. Ignatius wrote the *Spiritual Exercises*, a masterpiece of Christian spirituality. He used this book to direct people in retreats. His goal was always to help them know, love, and follow Christ more fully.

Today more than 16,000 Jesuit priests, brothers, and seminarians continue to serve Christ, the Church, and the world in high schools, colleges, parishes, and other ministries in more than 100 countries. The year 2013 marked another historic moment for the Society of Jesus. The Argentinean cardinal Jorge Bergoglio, S.J., was elected as head of the Catholic Church, taking the name Pope Francis. He is the first Jesuit ever to hold this office.

WHAT ARE THE *SPIRITUAL EXERCISES*?

Ignatius wrote the *Spiritual Exercises* over the course of several years. He began jotting notes, in Latin and Spanish, during his own conversion experience. At first, this notebook was just a set of insights and reflections based on his prayer, reading, experience, and conversation. He gradually edited, clarified, and organized these notes into a coherent spiritual program. He also began sharing his *Exercises* with others, guiding them through short, informal retreats to help them center their own lives in Christ. Later he trained his Jesuit brothers in this unique spiritual pathway, so that they, too, could lead other people through retreats. Writers sometimes speak of "Ignatian spirituality" when referring to all of the spiritual writings of St. Ignatius and his Jesuit followers.

Ignatius did little that was brand new; rather, he drew upon other saints and spiritual writers, taking the best of the Christian tradition and organizing it in a compelling way. His *Exercises* help us to grow in our spiritual lives by guiding us through reflections on Bible passages, Christian virtues, and related religious topics. In some sections of the *Exercises*, Ignatius plunges us into the mystery of sin and evil. In other parts, he helps us to contemplate the love and power of Christ by engaging our emotions and imaginations. A retreat with the *Spiritual Exercises* is an intensely personal experience, whereby we deepen our relationship with Christ.

SHOULD I JUST READ THE *SPIRITUAL EXERCISES*?

You can try. If you do, you'll probably feel frustrated and disappointed. Why? The *Exercises* are really a guidebook intended for retreat directors—those who are guiding others on a retreat. Ignatius wrote much of the *Spiritual Exercises* using technical and theological terms. His book was not meant to be read by a wide audience. Rather, Ignatius wanted Jesuits and other directors to adapt and apply the *Exercises*; he wanted them to help retreatants in a variety of contexts and situations. For almost five hundred years, Jesuits and other directors have done just that—guiding millions of retreatants around the world. As a disciple of Christ and a follower of St. Ignatius, I'm honored to be a part of this long and rich tradition, as I now present this version of the *Exercises* in the twenty-first century.

HOW CAN ST. IGNATIUS HELP ME?

Ignatian spirituality is uniquely suited to help busy people grow closer to Christ. Ignatius was a busy person, just like you. He traveled around Europe; he wrote and taught; he studied, prayed, and served the poor. He was a university student, a priest, and a spiritual director. Under the guidance of the Holy Spirit, he created a retreat to help busy people. It is a retreat for doctors, lawyers, students, seminarians, merchants, government leaders, parents, and people from all walks of life. His *Exercises* are designed with a flexible format. I have led people through silent retreats based on the *Exercises* over the course of thirty days, eight days, or a weekend. I've also helped people make the retreat in daily life over several days or weeks. That's what we'll be doing here: a retreat in daily life for the next ten days.

In a typical retreat (in the time of Ignatius and today), a retreatant listens to the preaching of a Jesuit each day or meets regularly with a trained spiritual director. The retreatant then takes time daily to pray about different themes and topics from the *Exercises*. As I said, there are many ways to make a retreat: by going to a retreat house, attending a series of talks at a church, or by using a book. You'll be using this book to guide you in your own personal retreat.

WHAT'S THE FORMAT OF THIS BOOK?

In this book, I'll describe a different topic in each of the ten Heart Exercises. I'll often use images related to the human heart because I find that this helps us to connect our emotions with our physical bodies and our spiritual lives. Jesus, too, has a living human heart that beats with love for each of us! Each of the topics will build on the ones that came before. Some topics will be classic themes from Christian life, as described by Ignatius: sin, forgiveness, creation, etc. Other chapters will help us to examine God's work in our own lives or will connect key gospel passages with our own experiences. I'll use personal examples to help illustrate the various topics.

This book will help you to deepen your relationship with Christ and pray in different ways, using the writings of Ignatius. Many Catholics are familiar with praying devotional prayers, such as the Rosary, and going to Mass. Christians from other churches may have their own traditions, such as reading from scripture or singing favorite hymns. These are all excellent ways to pray. In this retreat, we'll use and build on these classic methods. The topics and questions in this book will also draw us deeper into prayer. These exercises will invite personal reflection on our own lives and experiences. We'll also look at aspects of Jesus' life, and I'll ask you to prayerfully apply them to yourself.

When you pray with the questions at the end of each chapter, use a journal or notebook to jot down some thoughts and reflections; this will help you to engage the retreat more fully.

Hopefully, this retreat will help you to deepen a warm, ongoing, heart-to-heart relationship with Jesus.

In exercises 1, 2, and 3, we'll examine a few key spiritual themes from Ignatius and put these into practice. We'll begin with creation, spiritual awareness, and gratitude. These opening chapters will serve as "stretching" or "warm-up" exercises that will lead us into the meat of Ignatian spirituality. Most Jesuit retreat houses today follow a similar structure when leading people through eight-day retreats and weekend retreats. I have included some activities and questions at the end of each chapter; these will help you to reflect, pray, and apply these themes to your own life.

In exercise 4, we will walk through one of Ignatius's most famous reflections, the "First Principle and Foundation." There we'll consider God's plan for us and how to live this out in our daily routines. Exercise 5 will present an examination of conscience, a vital tool for growth in the spiritual life. Exercise 6 returns to the theme of gratitude, leading us to take a deeper look at our own gifts and talents. Exercise 7 considers some of our weaknesses and challenges as we try to walk with Christ in the world today. Exercise 8 examines the mysterious history of sin—in the world and in ourselves. In exercise 9, we explore God's mercy and forgiveness toward us. We'll finish with a reflection on the call of Christ—the King who calls sinners such as you and me to draw closer to him.

There are three brief "Pause for Heart Check" activities; you can find them after exercises 3 and 7 and following the

Conclusion. These are opportunities for brief check-ins during your retreat. In these pauses, you'll find a few questions to help you to review your notes and reflect on what has happened so far. The appendix offers a few additional prayers and resources to help you continue your spiritual journey with the Lord. You can use these during your retreat or afterward.

HOW SHOULD I USE THIS BOOK?

You can read and pray with one chapter of *Abide in the Heart of Christ* each day for ten days. It will take you twenty to thirty minutes to read each chapter and then another twenty to thirty minutes to reflect and pray. You might read in the morning and then pray in the evening. You may choose to spread out your retreat over several weeks—perhaps reading a chapter every other day or every Sunday. Do whatever works for you; it's a flexible retreat that is designed to fit your schedule and your needs.

I hope that my examples and reflections offer helpful guidance. But don't stop there! *Be sure that you pray!* Talk to Jesus; listen to him. Ignatius reminds us that we must allow the Lord our "Creator to deal directly with the creature and the creature with its Creator and Lord" (*Spiritual Exercises*, 15; hereafter *SE*).[1] Jesus is the true director of your retreat. He wants to draw you deeper into relationship with him. For hundreds of years, the Holy Spirit has used the writings of Ignatius to draw millions of people deeper into the love of Christ. This is what Christ wants for you, too.

The activities at the end of each chapter will ask you to participate in specific ways. For example, you may be invited to find a photo from your Baptism, to dig out a souvenir from a favorite vacation spot, or to reflect on your own gifts and talents. You can carry out these reflections alone or in a group. For example, you can do them with family or friends or with a Bible study group, service group, or retreat team. I've found that it is fruitful to first read a chapter and do the reflections alone and *then* to discuss the experience with others.

If you simply read this book, you'll certainly get something out of it. If you read and then think about the questions in each chapter, you'll get more. If you read and think and journal and pray, then you'll get all the grace that Christ wants to offer you.

LANGUAGE OF THE HEART

I've titled each exercise using language of the heart. For example, the first exercise is "A Heart Is Created," the second is "What's in My Heart?" and so on. Throughout Christian history, the heart has been a rich and powerful symbol for our spiritual lives. Our physical hearts are a muscle that must be exercised, stretched, and strengthened. The heart is a popular image of love, even in contemporary culture (e.g., I ❤ U, I ❤ NY). If I say I "love" New York or Italian food, I am really expressing a warm affection for these things. Of course, I love my family at a far deeper level; this is a love that flows from deep in my heart. This love involves affection as well as an ongoing commitment to their well-being. Real love is not always easy; we need God's help. He promises to renew our hearts: "I will remove the heart of stone from your flesh and give you a heart of flesh" (Ez 36:26).[2] For centuries, Christians have honored the Sacred Heart of Jesus; Jesus himself has a beating, human heart right now.

The eternal Son of God was conceived in the womb of the Virgin Mary; he grew as a boy and into a young man; he preached, taught, suffered, and died on the Cross; he rose to new life in his resurrected Body. The risen Jesus has a human heart that is beating with love for you and me right now. Jesus wants to draw us deeper into his grace and love each day. I hope this book will help you with that deepening, enabling you to live and walk more closely with Christ.

Here are a few quick points before we begin this retreat:

You'll need a Bible. There are many versions and translations to choose from. An online Bible or Bible app is fine, too.

You'll need a pen and a journal or notebook. You'll notice several questions at the end of each exercise and in the "Pause for Heart Check" sections. As you prayerfully answer these questions, jot down a few words in your journal. You can do this during or after your prayer. Writing will help you focus. If you prefer, you can type your reflections on your phone or laptop instead of using a paper notebook. It's a good idea to review your notes after your retreat as you work to continue your spiritual growth.

Find a quiet spot to pray each day. Use this spot each day for your prayer time, answering the reflection questions, and writing notes in your journal. Your quiet spot could be a chapel, your bedroom, or another peaceful place.

Choose a patron saint to walk with you during this retreat. You might call upon your guardian angel, St. Ignatius, the Blessed Mother, or another favorite saint. Ask this holy person to pray for you and help you to make a good retreat.

Pray for a specific grace. What do you want from the Lord? Why did you begin this retreat? Ask the Lord for what you want. Maybe you are feeling stressed and you want peace in your heart. Maybe you are seeking a sense of direction; perhaps you are looking for guidance as you approach an important crossroad in your life—considering a move to a new city or wondering what to do during your retirement. Maybe you want healing from the Lord; perhaps you've had a tough year and have made some poor decisions. Pray for grace. Trust that the Lord will give you what you need and even more besides.

During your retreat, do something extra. For instance, you might abstain from TV, social media, or the internet during your retreat to help you focus on the Lord. Or, you might attend morning Mass each day at a local parish. Taking some special action can help to foster a prayerful environment during your time of retreat.

You may be tempted to race through this book. *Go slowly instead.* Jesus himself took time in prayer; he often went to the Temple and into the desert. "He went up on the mountain by himself to pray" (Mt 14:23). Listen. Speak to Jesus. Don't rush.

It helps to repeat an exercise a second time. Or you might even spend another day in prayer on the same chapter of this retreat. Repetition helps us to pray better and dig deeper. As Ignatius says, "It is not by knowing much, but in relishing things interiorly, that satisfies the soul" (*SE*, 2). Go back to those parts that you found particularly inspiring and grace-filled. Don't gulp down your spiritual food; savor it and enjoy the graces.

It works if you work it. If you put your mind and heart into these exercises, then you will reap a rich harvest. Ignatius tells us to begin the *Spiritual Exercises* with great openness and generosity toward the Lord. The more we have a "great spirit and generosity toward our Creator and Lord . . . the more do we dispose ourselves to receive graces and gifts from his divine and supreme goodness" (*SE* 5, 20). Pray for an open heart. Then put your heart into this retreat and trust that Christ will renew it. For almost five hundred years, he's been doing just that for millions of people with the *Spiritual Exercises* of St. Ignatius. And now it's your turn.

Ready? Set? Let's go!

A Heart Is Created: God, Creation, and Me

God looked at everything he had made and

found it very good.

—Genesis 1:31

Put your hand on your heart. Feel. Wait for ten seconds. Listen. What do you hear? *Pum bum, pum bum.* Your heart is quietly giving you life at this very moment. It pumps life and blood through your body every day, every minute—and yet you might rarely notice this miracle. Your heart is a symbol of Christ's love for you. There he is—quietly, powerfully loving you. Giving you life and love. Pouring out his life and blood for you. Do you notice?

I notice my heart when it is pounding before a big presentation, when I see an old friend, when I'm running, and when

I'm excited, afraid, or overjoyed. *Ba-bum, ba-bum, ba-bum!* I notice these physical signs and so do you . . . sometimes. But what about spiritual signs? How can we notice Jesus' love for us more often and more deeply? Jesus made our hearts, and he wants us to notice his heart.

Who am I? What am I? Let these questions drift through your mind and heart. For example, I am a son, a brother, a priest, an American, a man, a friend, a teacher, and a sinner. Yet who am I really? St. Ignatius of Loyola points us to the truth of our human identity: we are beloved sons and daughters of God. He writes, "I will consider how God dwells in creatures . . . in human beings, giving us intelligence, and finally how in this way he dwells also in myself, giving me existence, life, sensation, and intelligence; and even further making me his temple, since I am created as a likeness and image of his divine majesty" (*SE*, 235). Ignatius points us to the opening chapter of Genesis. There we see the Father shaping, handcrafting Adam and Eve. The scriptures show us how the human race is the pinnacle of God's creation. God made us, and God sees that we are "very good" (Gn 1:31).

Since we are made in God's image, we are like God. We have an ability to know, understand, speak, listen, and love. God has all knowledge, and God *is* love; still, we share in his gifts in our own, human way. Our hearts are made in the image of the Sacred Heart of Jesus. His heart beats with love for us, even at this very moment. *Pum bum, pum bum.*

We aren't perfect, of course, but let's focus on how we resemble God in his goodness. Imagine God looking at you with joy and love. He is pleased. He did a good job, a "very good" job in fact. God looks upon your heart and smiles. What do you feel in your heart when you see God looking at you? Are you happy? Embarrassed? For many of us, seeing ourselves as made in the image of God is not easy, even though we are made for communion with the Lord. Yet the truth is that God desires a loving relationship with us in this life and in eternal life.

Our culture often emphasizes the things that are wrong with us. Advertisements constantly tell us we're not wealthy enough, not beautiful enough, not strong enough, and not cool enough. Yet sometimes we do get a glimpse of our true identity as beloved sons and daughters of the Father. I'll share an example from my own life when I experienced this truth.

LITTLE ADAM IN A RURAL EDEN

I grew up in the suburbs of St. Louis, Missouri, and my grandparents had a farm about an hour outside the city. As kids, my sister and I would often go there for a long weekend with Grandma and Granddad. I know my parents loved us, but I'm sure they were grateful to have a quiet weekend now and then while my sister and I were away in the country. For me, these trips were a little taste of Eden.

On a typical long weekend, my grandparents would pick us up on a Saturday morning. My grandfather drove one of those massive Buicks that were popular in the 1970s; it was like a giant green yacht on wheels. My sister, Katie, and I would run out of the house to the car with our bags. Mom and Dad would follow, hug us, and tell us to be good. We'd hug Grandma and Granddad, put the bags in the trunk, and slide onto that slick vinyl backseat. After a friendly honk that reverberated through the neighborhood, we'd be off.

An hour later, my sister and I would wake up in the backseat, just as the car started rumbling down the gravel road. An old country song played quietly on the radio. We'd see the red barn, the little bridge, and my grandparents' farmhouse. They still owned a house in the suburbs; this was their weekend place—a scenic spot for rest and recreation. The Buick would lurch slightly as Granddad pulled into the gravel driveway.

We'd grab our bags as Grandma opened the house. Granddad reached deeper into the trunk for their bags, along with a cooler and grocery bags. We had a familiar ritual of quickly unpacking and immediately suggesting foods for my grandma to make: "Fried chicken! Apple pie! Bacon and eggs!" Grandma promised to make all of our favorites, as usual. But first she wanted to look at the garden with my sister, while my granddad and I went to the barn to check on the animals.

Grandpa was tall and lanky, as I am now; back then I was a pudgy kid with a mess of brown hair. He could have walked faster, but he went slowly so that I could keep up, taking three steps for every one of his. As we walked, he'd stop to point out little details in nature. As we crossed the creek, he said, "See here, JW." This was his nickname for me, the initials of my first and middle name, Joseph William. "Right here, these little fish. Those aren't really fish. They're tadpoles. They'll get bigger and turn into frogs." I had heard this from my science teacher in school, but seeing them with Granddad made it alive and real. After poking around in the stream with a stick for a minute, he continued. "And here, see this pink flower? Well, that flower will turn into an apple. And then we can pick them, and your grandma can make them into a nice apple pie." He'd also ask me about my classes at school, my baseball team, and my parents. We'd continue our journey together to the barn, and then head to the fish pond.

As I look back on it, these weekends with my grandparents were a kind of rural Eden. I was like a little eight-year-old Adam, with my grandpa as a loping God the Father. He took time with me. He literally bent down to speak at my level. He did not create apple trees, but he did cultivate and care for them. I am literally made in my grandfather's likeness, as I resemble him in my appearance and temperament. In the same way, God has made all of us in his very image and likeness, giving us qualities that he himself possesses.

Sometimes we simply need a place of quiet to see the Lord and to see ourselves more clearly. For me, it was the quiet and beauty of my grandparents' country home and the patient attention of my grandfather that granted me this perspective. A retreat can also offer a place of peace, where we set aside the busy confusion of daily life. Even a ten-day retreat in daily life can be an opportunity to receive the peace and grace that we seek.

JESUS SAYS, "COME AWAY BY YOURSELVES TO A DESERTED PLACE AND REST A WHILE" (MK 6:31)

We all seek peace and rest, but they aren't always easy to find. Often, we need a change from our daily routines to find them. It's not that daily life is bad, but it somehow dulls our senses. After a weekend with my grandparents, I returned to school the next week refreshed and renewed. I was more attentive in science class; I was kinder to my sister who shared the joyful trip with me. I had a deeper sense of gratitude for my family, myself, and the Lord who made me.

Jesus sends out his disciples to preach and teach. They come back and tell him "all that they had done and taught" (Mk 6:30). Then Jesus invites them to "come away by yourselves to a deserted place and rest" (Mk 6:31). Ignatius encourages us to take time away for a retreat. So often we have "our mind divided among many matters"; we are renewed when we can "concentrate instead all our attention on one alone, namely, the service of our Creator and our own spiritual progress" (*SE*, 20). We need to reflect on what we have done and what has happened. We need quiet time alone with Jesus, away from the busyness of towns and cities.

Jesus sent us out to work, to study, to help our families. And he says, "I will give you rest. Come away by yourselves." On retreat, Christ can cultivate his relationship with us, so that it can flourish and bear great fruit. To be with him, we must leave certain things behind. We need to set aside email, phone calls, television, and other distractions. Even thirty to sixty minutes can make a big difference.

You have begun this ten-day retreat because you, too, seek a place of peace and rest. Jesus has invited you to come away with him on this retreat—and you said yes. A retreat, even one in the midst of our daily routines, is an opportunity to encounter the heart of Christ. In the quiet, we can hear his heart beat. We can hear our own hearts, too. This can be disconcerting, even alarming. We crave his peace and yet, paradoxically, at the same time we fear being in his presence! Again, hear our Savior's gentle invitations to you: "Come away with me," and "Learn from me, for I am meek and humble of heart" (Mt 11:29). Our hearts are restless; they find rest with his Sacred Heart.

QUESTIONS AND ACTIVITIES

1. Go to your prayer spot, and sit in a comfortable place to begin your time of prayer. Begin by saying one of the prayers found in the appendix: perhaps the Morning Offering or the *Anima Christi*.

2. Put your hand on your heart. Recall that God made your heart, and it is very good. Keep your hand there for thirty beats. How are you feeling right now? Write a brief description in your journal; describe both your physical and emotional states. Are you happy, tired, sad or something else? Tell Jesus about this: "Lord, right now I feel . . . " Is there anything the Lord wants to say to you?

3. Read Genesis 1:26–31, and imagine God's new creation. Picture the green plants, breathe in the fresh air, and feel the peace of God's handiwork.

4. Imagine God joyfully forming you as a tiny child in your mother's womb and his knowledge that even before your birth, you were already "very good." How do you think your parents felt when they learned that your mother was pregnant with you? How do you feel as you imagine yourself newly created by God?

5. My grandparents' farm was a holy place for me. Is there a holy place that you have encountered in your life? This might be a favorite vacation spot, a trip to Rome, or a previous retreat. Recall this place in your mind. Remember the sights, sounds, smells, and people. How did you feel when you were there? How was God present to you in this place? Jot down a few words describing this holy place and your experiences there.

What's in My Heart?
Awareness and Emotion

I will remove your heart of stone and

give you a heart of flesh.

—Ezekiel 36:26

"Shields up!" Captain Kirk shouts to Scotty, after seeing their enemy, the Romulans, appear on the view screen.

"Aye, aye, Captain!" Scotty responds.

This familiar scene from Star Trek also occurs in numerous books and films. Here come the bad guys—get ready! Perhaps we live our lives in a similar way, telling ourselves, "Get ready! Brace yourself! Keep a stiff upper lip!" We may reflexively tense up as we prepare for the next test, competition, presentation, or argument. "Shields up!" After a while, we may leave our shields permanently up, so that we won't get hurt.

But after months or years of stress and pressure, the shields almost become part of our hearts. We feel numb and hardened as we defend ourselves in daily battles, real or imagined. "What's in my heart?" It's a question that can be hard to answer. We may ignore our emotions or simply forget them; they may seem to get in the way of the next project or battle.

How am I feeling right now? Take a moment to reflect on that question. Let's begin with a physical assessment. Are you standing or sitting? Tired, sick, energetic, or hungry? Start with the top of your head and slowly move down your body. Is your neck sore from staring at a computer all day? Is your back tired from standing for hours? Maybe you're smiling because you've had a really great morning. How about your elbows, hands, lower back, legs, knees, and feet? Maybe today has been a quiet, peaceful day and your're feeling pretty good. Maybe it hasn't, and your're feeling exhausted.

As Ignatius reminded us, we are truly temples of the Holy Spirit. God made us, including our bodies. If we are feeling good, then we want to thank God for this grace. If we are hurting, then we want to ask God for help and blessings. "Ask God our Lord for what I want and desire," writes Ignatius (*SE*, 47). *What do I want? What do I desire?* At different points in the *Spiritual Exercises*, Ignatius invites us to pray for joy, gratitude, generosity, and sorrow for sin. But before we voice these prayers, we must first be aware of what we are experiencing—physically, emotionally, and spiritually. We will need God's help to become more aware of what is happening in us.

After reflecting on our bodies, let's move to our emotions. *Am I in a good mood? Am I joyful, or upset and anxious?* We may want to ask for Christ's help, to help us see and hear what is in our hearts. Imagine Jesus looking at you and asking, "How are you doing?" He listens attentively and patiently. Perhaps you again feel resistant, thinking, *Jesus knows everything, right? Doesn't he already know how I am feeling?* Yes, he does. *But do I know how I am feeling? Perhaps I don't.* Talking it through with Christ can help you to know how you are doing.

Finish this sentence: "Jesus, right now I am feeling . . ." The heart of Jesus can help you to get in touch with your own heart.

In a real battle, shields can be helpful. The problem is that we tend to leave these shields up. Over time, they can separate us from others, from God, and even from ourselves. We desire communion with God and others, but these shields and defenses can get in the way. To be aware of our emotions and experience, we must lower our defenses and open our hearts to the Lord. We must lower our shields and talk with Jesus.

"A HEART OF FLESH" (EZ 36:26)

Jesus is truly God and truly human—he is like us in all things but sin. He experienced emotions like ours when he walked this earth. In fact, he has a risen body right now. His Sacred Heart pours out love for us at every moment. In the gospels, we see Jesus in times of joy, sorrow, and anger. He rejoices in his Father's faithfulness: "I give you praise, Father, Lord of heaven and earth" (Lk 10:21). He weeps at the tomb of his close friend,

Lazarus (Jn 11:35). Jesus sees the merchants encroaching on the Temple, and overturning their tables, he commands, "Stop making my Father's house a marketplace" (Jn 2:16).

In the Incarnation, Jesus enters into the fullness of our human experience. He does not detach himself from human emotion, like some sort of stoic philosopher. He feels deeply because he loves deeply. He is a passionate Savior. He is not a slave to emotion, but he draws on his feelings as part of his mission. He undergoes his Passion with a depth of love for his Father and all humanity. In paintings of the Sacred Heart, his heart is often portrayed as on fire, as he burns with love for us. His heart is also wounded: on the Cross, the soldier's lance pierces Christ's heart, and blood and water flow out. Jesus knows sorrow and pain; however, his heart is not destroyed. Rather, it breaks open, to pour out love and grace all the more.

SERVING IN HONDURAS

My training as a Jesuit has taken me to many places. My novitiate was in St. Paul, Minnesota; I studied philosophy in Chicago, Illinois, taught high school in Denver, Colorado, and served at a parish in Belize in Central America. Every one of these assignments has held both joy and suffering, and in each assignment, I've done my best to avoid the suffering. It has never worked.

When I was a Jesuit seminarian, I led a group of boys from Regis Jesuit High School in Colorado on a service trip to Honduras. There we worked at the children's nutrition clinic in a rural village. Each day we helped the staff care for two dozen malnourished children, all between the ages of two and seven. They were all small for their ages; some were skinny and tired. They ate four to five times each day, with baths, naps, and story time in between. My students were generous, patient, and caring; the children were beautiful. After only a few days, we could see a difference; they began smiling and talking more as they gained weight and strength. The staff was warm and welcoming as they allowed us to join in their holy work. There were plenty of joyful times: singing, laughing, dancing with the kids, and making jokes with the boys in my group.

Yet there was suffering, too. It was summer, and more than 100 degrees and humid most days. The students and I felt tired and nauseated almost the entire trip, as we ate unusual foods and dealt with unfamiliar surroundings (tongue tacos and chicken-foot soup were among the local delicacies!). I spoke some Spanish; I could communicate about as well as an average Honduran eight-year-old. These limitations were humbling, even embarrassing. Suffering scares me; I run. When it does find me, it hurts. Yet when we unite our suffering with Christ's, this pain can also stretch our hearts. My heart grew as I saw the daily routine of the poor in the surrounding town. I was there for only two weeks; this is their world every day.

These challenges offered an opportunity to trust in Christ more fully. In some ways, I had no choice! He continued to invite me to listen, to receive help, and to offer help. I remember helping the staff to wash the children's hands and faces before and after meals; I smiled and they smiled back. I watched the boys playing soccer with the kids, everyone laughing and having fun, showing me that laughs and smiles translate across languages and cultures.

I've experienced other kinds of suffering as a seminarian, including confusion, anxiety, and disappointment: learning can be hard, and studying Spanish or ancient philosophy is not easy. As a college campus minister, I've shared conversations with students as they discussed broken relationships, spiritual doubts, and anxieties. *Compassion* literally means "to suffer with" someone. Of course, I've had blessings in these assignments, too: as a high school teacher, I celebrated my students' progress, relaxed when weeks-long research projects were submitted, and laughed at their goofy teenage humor.

Throughout my time as a Jesuit, I've had plenty of joys and sufferings. I've recognized the joys as blessings. And I've learned that God does not want us to seek suffering for its own sake. He asks us to love Christ and his people, and we acknowledge that suffering will be part of our journey with him. If we keep praying and keep talking with Christ, this suffering can make our hearts bigger and stronger, and give us a greater capacity to love. I cried in Honduras; I turned to Christ and he showed me that my suffering was a gift from him. In my confusion and sickness, I got a small taste of the daily struggles that the poor children experience. I saw Jesus at work in the generosity of the staff and volunteers: through them, he fed these tiny beautiful children, strengthening them with food and love.

"I will remove the heart of stone from your flesh and give you a heart of flesh," says the Lord (Ez 36:26). This is a scary prophesy. A heart made of stone looks strong and unbreakable. We're calm, cool, in control, and unbeatable. But is this what we really want? A stone heart is actually quite fragile because it can chip and shatter; it's dead, not alive. A heart of flesh is living, moving, and beating. The heart of Jesus is living, bleeding, on fire. We must risk being hurt to be in love. And we probably will get hurt. But Christ can heal our wounds. Those close to Jesus receive hearts that are more and more like his heart.

The two disciples on the road to Emmaus cry out, "Were not our hearts burning [within us]" (Lk 24:32) when the risen Christ speaks to them on their journey. Those who hear St. Peter's preaching were "cut to the heart"; they wanted to change their lives and follow Jesus (Acts 2:37).

Pray: "Lord, I am afraid of having my heart broken. But I do want to allow my heart to be broken open, as yours is open to us. Give me a heart like yours that can receive love and give love."

QUESTIONS AND ACTIVITIES

1. Begin with one of the prayers from the appendix.

2. In your journal, complete each of these sentences in two to three lines:

   Lord, physically, right now I am feeling . . .
   Lord, emotionally, right now I am feeling . . .

> Lord, here are a few thoughts that have been on my mind today . . .

3. Read Mark 10:16 (Jesus blesses the children) or John 11:32–35 (Jesus learns that Lazarus has died). Focus on Jesus' emotions. How does he feel in this passage? Ask him! How do you feel as you watch him?

4. Recall one time you felt sad, one time you felt angry, and one time you felt loved. Briefly describe each of these in your journal.

5. What is one experience that has brought you joy? Perhaps it was a hiking trip to Colorado, seeing a friend's smile, or preparing a meal for your family. Reflect on how God was active in this experience. Did you feel him in the beauty of creation, or in the warmth of a friendship?

A Grateful Heart: My Spiritual Top 10

Blessed are your eyes, because they see, and

your ears, because they hear!

—Matthew 13:16

When I was an undergraduate at Saint Louis University, I majored in communication because my dream job was being an anchorman on ESPN's *SportsCenter*. At SLU, I was immersed in campus media: I covered sports for the school newspaper, my roommate and I did play-by-play commentary for the men's basketball team on KSLU radio, and I watched a lot of ESPN. A whole lot. Even now, as a busy priest, I still turn on ESPN a few times each week. My favorite part of *SportsCenter* has always been the "Top 10 Plays" feature. For those not in the know, this segment of the show delivers the best and most amazing

highlights from the day in sports from dozens of games in a
hundred cities throughout hours of competition. We see out-
fielders diving for catches, point guards making slam dunks,
and eighty-yard touchdown passes from quarterbacks. Someone
(probably a communication major!) sat down and reviewed the
day's footage to give us a few key athletic moments.

MY TOP 10

Highlight reels capture the best moments in sports. What about
your own Top 10? Your *spiritual* Top 10? When have you felt
close to God? You may not have photos or videos of all of these,
but you certainly have images and memories embedded in your
mind and heart. These aren't simply fun events—such as winning fifty dollars in the lottery. Recall a few special moments
when you felt peace, love, and communion with Christ. For
most of us, one or two examples will jump out immediately.

One of my Top 10 moments is the day I was ordained to
the priesthood. My whole family was there at the St. Francis
Xavier College Church on SLU's campus, as were many Jesuit
priests and friends from high school and college; there were
beautiful flowers, music, and powerful prayer. It was especially
meaningful to be back at SLU, where my Jesuit vocation had
begun to take root.

The church is a beautiful, massive stone structure, and the
high, colorful stained-glass windows portray scenes from the
lives of Christ and Jesuit saints. During the Mass, the church
was alive with light and movement. The choir, the archbishop,

hundreds of Jesuits, and my family and friends raised their voices to the Lord throughout a two-hour liturgy of praise. One of my Jesuit mentors, Fr. Rich Buhler, helped me don my priestly vestments for the very first time. I was exhausted, exhilarated, and at peace. I felt a tangible, close communion with Christ and everyone attending the Mass.

What's in your Top 10? You might recall your Confirmation, college graduation, a family trip to Florida, your wedding day, or the day you won a state championship.

In the Catholic Church, we mark seven of these holy moments as sacraments. The sacraments include Baptism, Marriage, Holy Orders, and the Anointing of the Sick. If you were baptized as a baby, you may not consciously remember this day; but you can still picture it. You've probably seen photos. You know who your godparents are and maybe the priest who baptized you, and you've seen the church. With your intellect, memory, and imagination, you can visually and emotionally reconstruct events from the past. The Holy Spirit can help you to feel joy and gratitude as you recall these experiences in your mind. When thinking of your Baptism, envision your mom and dad as new parents—smiling, joyful, praying, and perhaps nervous. No doubt they asked God to bless this beautiful child—you!

BIBLICAL TOP 10

The Bible is a collection of God's actions in human history. The Bible highlights certain key moments in God's relationship with us. In the book of Exodus, we see the Israelites working as slaves to build the pyramids; then God calls to Moses in the burning bush. There are plagues of frogs and locusts, then the Passover feast and the parting of the Red Sea. Obviously, Exodus doesn't show us every single moment from the life of Moses: "On Thursday morning he went to the market and bought some radishes. He ran into an old friend there. Then he went home to take a nap. . . ." The Bible shows us God's love through key events in the lives of his people. All of this reaches a high point in the life of Christ. In him, God speaks and acts with power and authority, and those who encounter him are changed forever: the woman at the well, the blind, and the apostles.

Scripture teaches us how to see ourselves and our lives. Through the biblical narratives, the Holy Spirit invites us to reflect on our own experiences: How is God at work in this situation? What grace is the Lord offering me in this moment? Of course, God is at work in the world at every moment. But, we tend to notice his action in certain important events. We see this in scripture, in Christian history, and in our own lives.

ATTITUDE OF GRATITUDE

St. Ignatius invites us to prayerfully "ask for interior knowledge of all the great good I have received, in order that, stirred to profound gratitude I may become able to love and serve the Divine Majesty in all things" (*SE*, 233). We ask God to help us to see these gifts and thank him for them. If we give ourselves a little time for prayer and reflection, we can recall grace-filled events from own lives. We can even taste them again by revisiting them in our memories. The Holy Spirit can remind us of the beautiful things God has done in our lives. These blessings from the past can renew us in the present and give us renewed strength to trust the Lord in the future. But let's admit it, this is hard! Our minds tend to focus on the next event, the next deadline, and the stress that awaits us if we are late. Worse, on our own, we may often go back to our Bottom 10 instead of God's Top 10 in our lives. We can counteract these negative impulses. With God's help, we can cultivate an attitude of gratitude.

Let's look at a few good habits that we already have in this area. What hangs on the walls in most homes and apartments? Photos of family and friends as we like to recall people we love and the good times we shared together. What photos do we tend to keep on our phones? Usually it's joyful scenes with friends and family—maybe at a party, on vacation, or enjoying a meal. We can call these "sacramental moments." They may not be among the seven official sacraments of the Church, but they flow from the sacraments and lead us back to them. A good meal and conversation with close friends can be eucharistic. A good meal doesn't take the place of the Eucharist. Rather, Sunday Eucharist cultivates and opens my heart to receive Christ's love on the other six days of the week. A long hike up a summit in Colorado can bring a glimpse of God's glory—as Moses saw his glory on the mountaintop and the apostles saw Jesus' Transfiguration. Christ gives us joyful experiences as signs and symbols of his action in our lives.

How can I experience more of these sacramental moments? How can I cultivate an attitude of gratitude in my heart? The activities below offer a few suggestions. We may have to work at it at first, but the more we thank God, the more we'll notice even more blessings in our lives. Jesus tells us, "Blessed are your eyes, because they see, and your ears, because they hear!" (Mt 13:16). This is a way of sharpening our spiritual vision by practice. If we keep our heads down and eyes down, just stumbling through the day, then we're unlikely to see grace at work in our lives. If we are on the lookout for God's gifts, we are likely to see them.

You may find that you're often thanking God for the same things over and over, such as gratitude for the gift of life, family and friends, a warm house, or faith in Christ. It's okay to thank God again and again for the same gifts. In fact, we should never get tired of reviewing the blessings in our lives; God never gets tired of seeing our joy and receiving our gratitude. For example, my grandmother loves her grandchildren, loves talking about us, and loves showing off photos of us. She celebrates the blessings of life and family that God has given her. Her joyful gratitude is contagious; when I see her joy, I start to feel it, too! Gratitude never gets old—even if we're often thanking God for the same people, events, and other gifts.

Maybe you're already recoiling at this suggestion of spending intentional time on gratitude. *Can't it just be spontaneous? I want to rejoice and be thankful when the moment is right—not on some strict schedule*, you may think. I support spontaneity; however, oddly enough, spontaneity is connected to structure.

For me, when I deliberately make time each day to thank the Lord, I find that I am more apt to spontaneously notice holy moments as they are happening. I won't claim to be a pro at this, but I've certainly improved over the years. As I take time to look back at how God has been at work in my life, I can perceive similar events in my daily experience. I think, *Wait, there's that feeling again. Something about this conversation feels holy and good. Thank you, Lord. Help me to stay in the moment and not run away!*

What are your Top 10 spiritual moments when you felt close to the Lord? When I felt close to Christ, I know that his heart leapt for joy as he gave me this gift of his grace. My heart warms again and again as I recall these holy experiences.

QUESTIONS AND ACTIVITIES

1. What are your spiritual Top 10 moments, the times when you felt close to God? Give a brief description for each. Tell a friend about your Top 10. You may want to tear this page out of your journal and frame your list! You might even leave space to add *more*. (Top 12? Top 20?)

2. If you are artistic, then you could decorate your Top 10 list. Use colorful markers, paint, or whatever media you want. Frame it and hang it up. For the less artistic, you might just put a copy of it in your wallet or the top drawer of your desk. Look at it the next time you're having a tough day. Thank

the Lord for his gifts. Trust that he has more good in store
for you.

3. Find a photo or memento for one or two of these events.
    For example, you might dig out your baptismal certificate
    or look through your wedding photos. Ask the Holy Spirit
    to help you to remember the sights, sounds, smells, and
    emotions of that day. As you savor this moment, thank the
    Lord for his gift.

4. If possible, visit one of the places on your Top 10. This could
    be the church where you were baptized, a café where you've
    met friends, or the park where you proposed to your spouse,
    for example. Ask the Holy Spirit to give you a grateful heart
    as you savor the sights, smells, emotions, and graces of that
    place.

5. In prayer, have a short, friendly conversation with Jesus.
    He has been active in every one of your Top 10 moments. Is
    there anything you want to say to him? Anything you hear
    him saying to you?

Pause for Heart Check

You've completed three Heart Exercises. Congratulations! Now is a good opportunity to take a break and do a quick heart check. You could take a few minutes to pause for this heart check right now. Or you might choose to do this just before you begin exercise 4. Or if you have time, you could even take a full day to review the first three chapters of this book, look through your notes, and savor the graces you have received.

This is an opportunity to review what has happened on your retreat so far. It's like a brief team meeting after the first quarter of a football game or the school principal gathering the teachers together before Thanksgiving break. What has the Lord been doing? How have you responded? What are the highlights so far? The low points? What's working? What's not?

St. Ignatius recommends that we take time to review our prayer. This helps us to "notice and dwell on those points where I felt greater consolation or desolation, or had a greater spiritual experience" (*SE*, 62). What is the Lord doing in your heart? Thank him for these graces! Do you need to make any changes before you continue? For example, perhaps you try to pray in bed and keep falling asleep during prayer!

Here are a few questions for your prayerful consideration. You may want to jot down a few reflections in your journal.

1. How is your retreat going so far?

2. Are you taking time for daily prayer and journaling?

3. How has the Lord been active in your heart during this retreat? (Are you experiencing peace, joy, etc.?)

4. Briefly read through the reflections you've written in your journal.

5. Name two or three highlights from your retreat so far. Be specific.

6. Is there one section that you'd like to go back to—perhaps a scripture passage, a question, or an encounter with Jesus? You might take some time to pray with that section again.

7. Do you notice any areas where you are resisting, or holding back in your retreat? For example, are you having a hard time seeing God's gifts in your life? Name this resistance, and talk with the Lord about it.

8. Are there any changes you need to make before you begin exercise 4? What are they?

A Heart Centered in the Lord: The First Principle and Foundation

We are created to praise, reverence,

and serve God our Lord, and by

this means to save our souls.

—*Spiritual Exercises*, 23

Think of the exercises in the first three chapters of this book as warm-up activities. Think of them as stretching or calisthenics before the start of a longer workout. A singer may practice with musical scales and breathing exercises. All of this helps to get the heart pumping and the blood moving. All Jesuits do a thirty-day silent Ignatian retreat in our first year in the order. My superior led us in three "disposition days" before our thirty-day retreat began. You might be wondering, *Wait,* three extra days *of retreat before* thirty days *of retreat?!* I thought the same thing. It's true. However, this is simply spiritual common sense, rooted in the wisdom of St. Ignatius. We all need time to prepare. We'll move into the meat of our retreat now, using Ignatius's "First Principle and Foundation" (hereafter P&F).

THE P&F IN MY LIFE

I don't know about you, but I can spend a lot of time and energy running around trying to please others, meet their expectations, and achieve worldly success. Yet over time, all this leads to anxiety and frustration. I can easily forget that God's expectations for me are simpler and easier. I have to follow the requirements of my Jesuit superiors and bosses, of course, but I don't have to meet everybody else's shifting expectations for me. All I have to do is follow God's will. Yes, it's that simple. But sometimes it can be hard to know what is God's will for us!

We all make decisions every day, some big and some small. Should I go to the store after work or wait until this weekend? Should we move into a new house? Should I get a new job? What's the best decision? And how do I decide what to do? On many occasions, the P&F has helped me to make important decisions in my life. It's like a compass in my heart that I can check whenever I need to. Very concretely, it helps me to align my decisions with God's priorities.

Some decisions are pretty easy and don't require a lot of thought. I can simply realize I have time, so I'll pop into the store on the way home today. The bigger decisions, such as moving or looking for a new job, are not so easy. The P&F helps me to set my sights on the Lord and walk in his light each day. I know deep in my heart that my life will be better, more peaceful, and healthier if I make decisions according to God's plan for me. The opposite is also true. My life gets stressful, unhealthy, and out of whack when I do not live according to God's plan.

WHAT IS THE P&F?

In the P&F, Ignatius summarizes the purpose and goal of human life in a few short lines. He then invites us to apply it to ourselves and our daily activities. As we look over the P&F, we'll ask the Lord to help us center our hearts on him. We all want to follow Christ, most of the time. Sometimes we resist. The P&F points us back to the true goal of human life, which is the true goal of my life, too. Ignatius packs a lot into a few lines; we'll reflect on the P&F in the next few pages. Here it is:

Principle & Foundation

We are created to praise, reverence, and serve
> God our Lord,
and by this means to save our souls.

The other things on the face of the earth are
> created for us

to help us in attaining the end for which we are
　　　created: to praise, reverence, and serve
　　　God our Lord, and by this means save
　　　our souls.

Hence, we are to make use of them in as far as
　　　they help us
in the attainment of this end, and we must rid
　　　ourselves of them
in as far as they prove a hindrance to us [in
　　　fulfilling our purpose] to praise, rev-
　　　erence, and serve God our Lord, and
　　　by this means save our souls.

Therefore, we must make ourselves indifferent
　　　to all created things,
as far as we are allowed free choice and are not
　　　under any prohibition.
Consequently, as far as we are concerned,
we should not prefer health to sickness, riches
　　　to poverty,
honor to dishonor, a long life to a short life.
The same holds for all other things.
Our one desire and choice should be what is
　　　more conducive
to the end for which we are created (*SE,* 23).[3]

GOD'S PLAN AND MY RESPONSE

In the P&F, Ignatius draws on scripture and Christian tradition to help us reflect on the ultimate goal of each man and woman: eternal life with Christ. This is "the end for which we are created." Ignatius does not think that he is saying anything new; he is simply summarizing centuries of Christian thought. The greatest commandment, Jesus says, is to "love the Lord, your God, with all your heart, with all your soul, and with all your mind" (Mt 22:37). Older folks may even remember the questions posed by the *Baltimore Catechism* they used in Catholic grammar school: "Who made me? God made me. Why did God make me?" Ignatius replies, "To know, love and serve him in this world and to be happy with him forever in heaven." Simple enough.

"To save our souls" is a rich and beautiful phrase from Ignatius. God wants us to be with him in heaven forever. Our time on earth is a preparation before we reach our heavenly home. In a sense, heaven begins now for those who love God, live in his love, and love others as themselves. The saints lived this way: despite many difficulties and obstacles, they lived in the truth of Christ. Some may ask, "But can we save ourselves? I thought that only Christ could save us?" A full answer would demand a much longer discussion that is beyond the scope of our retreat. Certainly Ignatius believes that God saves us; we do not save ourselves. However, God invites us to actively cooperate with him. The Lord calls us to live a life of faith, hope, and love—and he gives us many supports and helps to do this. Ignatius wants us to reflect deeply on our response to God's divine plan: "How am I responding to the Lord?"

Ignatius continues, "The other things on the face of the earth are created for us to help us in attaining the end (goal) for which we are created. Hence, we are to make use of them in as far as they help us in the attainment of this end, and we must rid ourselves of them in as far as they prove a hindrance to us." What does Ignatius mean by this? He reminds us that God is good and that God has created the world in goodness and love. Recall our reflections on Genesis and creation in the first exercise: God's grace flows into the created world and human life, and we are invited to be good stewards of these gifts and use them to the best of our ability.

For example, we should eat healthy foods to feel strong and energetic. We should walk or get other exercise to keep our bodies fit. Reading books, having conversations with friends, making time for prayer, etc.—all of these things help us to live healthy, fruitful, and meaningful lives. These actions help us to flourish and experience lasting friendship with God. However, there are certain things we may need to minimize or avoid, to "rid ourselves" of. These include excessive consumption of food or alcohol. If I am allergic to poison ivy, then I should be cautious when I am in the woods. If I tend to speed when I am late, then I should reevaluate my schedule so that I can leave on time. Maybe I need to use technology in daily life, but do I sometimes cling to my phone so that I can avoid interacting with others?

INDIFFERENCE?

So far so good. Ignatius continues, "Therefore, we must make ourselves indifferent to all created things, as far as we are allowed free choice and are not under any prohibition. Consequently, as far as we are concerned, we should not prefer health to sickness, riches to poverty, honor to dishonor . . ." This is where many of us may slam on the brakes. We shout, "What?! Ignatius are you crazy? Don't all of us seek health, wealth, and honor? Ok, maybe a few saints (like you, Ignatius) do not. But, c'mon! Be realistic!" Ignatius calmly points us back to the first line. What's the meaning of life? It's to love and serve God. Everything else on earth is for this purpose.

We can live out this simple purpose each day, no matter what. Living a life centered on Christ brings communion. Living through him, with him, and in him has tangible real-world consequences. A man might say, "I want to be rich!" However, there is no magic wand to grant his wish. He can work hard, invest wisely, and limit his expenses. Many other things are only partly within his control. Circumstances can happen that can thwart his goal. The economy dips. His wages are cut. Or he becomes ill and cannot work as many hours. This man has done nothing wrong. There is no "sin" in his failure to become rich. This is likewise true for health and reputation and a long lifespan. We can each do our part to stay healthy, but serious illnesses can arrive at any time; we can act honorably but still have our reputations damaged by gossip or social media.

We can't control everything. Here is what we can control: keeping our hearts centered on the Lord at all times—in health and sickness, in wealth and poverty. Married couples might notice that Ignatius's P&F is very similar to their wedding vows! A man and woman commit to each other, "For better or for worse, in sickness and in health, for richer or for poorer . . ." God's commitment to us is unconditional, so our commitment to the Lord should also be unconditional. Ignatius invites us to say, "Lord, no matter what happens, I will love and serve you. I'll surely experience both joys and sufferings in this life; no matter what, I will try to keep my eyes on you each day."

Again, maybe you feel a mix of emotions as you read these words. Many of us often say, "Yes, Lord, but . . ." We're drawn to Christ, yet we're dragging our feet. "Lord, can't I be with you just in 'better' and 'richer' and 'health'?" Be aware of those places in your heart where you are holding back. Talk with Jesus about these things. Be honest. And listen.

A MIND AND HEART OPEN TO THE LORD

Two more points. First, Ignatius means something very specific when he asks us to be "indifferent." In our daily speech, this word has a negative connotation. For example, imagine if a vegetarian friend offers us two options for lunch. I might respond, "Hmm. A tofu hotdog or a veggie burger? I'm indifferent. They both look awful." However, Ignatius intends us to have an open mind and heart, whatever comes our way. He points us toward an attitude of hope and trust in God. I am free; I have many good options before me. I could live in Missouri or Illinois; I could volunteer at a school or a homeless shelter; this Saturday I could go for a hike or meet a friend for brunch. I should strive to be indifferent: "Lord, however I can serve you best—that's what I want to do!"

By living with proper indifference, we can prevent ourselves from getting hung up on unimportant details and negotiating with God. For example, some may say, "Lord, I want to love and serve you. But I'd really prefer to do this on a beach and be famous and not have any health problems." Perhaps this is exactly what God has in store for you. Then again, maybe it's not. We are called to accept God's will for us, and not demand that he accept our will instead.

Second, Ignatius reminds us that certain things are forbidden, and thus off limits. The Ten Commandments apply, as do the Church's moral teachings, and legitimate civil laws. We should be free and indifferent—but there are obvious limits to our choices. For instance, you may notice that a certain charity really needs money to help poor children. A misguided Christian might think, "Aha! I know! I can just rob a bank and donate to the charity!" No, sorry: "You shall not steal." You can't do something bad even to do something good. Or perhaps a single woman thinks, "Wow, that guy is a great husband and father. Maybe I can seduce him so that he becomes my husband instead!" Again, nope. Off limits: "You shall not commit adultery." However, there are many, many places in life where we do have several valid options. For example, a young woman could pursue professions in education, law, art, or business. A man who has received a large sum of money could spend it on his family, donate it to the poor, give it to the Church, or invest it. This woman and man can simply recall the goal of life ("to praise, reverence, and serve God our Lord") and maintain a healthy indifference to everything else, so that they can attain this goal.

In the P&F, Ignatius gives us a succinct and compelling vision of life. He invites us to ponder these words and apply them to our own lives. Many of us also need to ask God for help to reorient our lives based on these ancient truths. Let us honestly ask, "Where is my heart in all of this? Lord, are my eyes on you? Or am I focused mainly on creating a cushy life centered on myself?" The P&F helps me to have a heart that is centered in the heart of Christ each day.

QUESTIONS AND ACTIVITIES

1. What would the world be like if more people followed the P&F? While driving? At school or in the workplace? Give an example.

2. What would my life be like if I followed the P&F more fully? For example . . .

    a. Lord, my heart is open to your will in these two areas of my life: ____" (e.g., my level of wealth, type of job, city I live in, etc.).

b. "Lord, I'm not so open to you in these areas of my life: _____" (e.g., my entertainment choices, health practices, popularity, etc.).

3. Rewrite the P&F in your own words. Don't change the meaning, but rewrite it to make it personal for yourself. You may want to write it from God's perspective: "I created you to praise, love, and serve me and my people; by doing this, you will go to heaven where you will rejoice with me forever . . ."

4. Post your P&F in your bedroom, office, or locker. Read it every day for a week. Use it for prayer: "Lord, if this is the goal you wish for my life, help me to live it today." And, "Lord, how did I live my P&F today? How did I fail to live it?"

A Reflective Heart: Examination of Conscience

Give thanks to the LORD, for he is

good, his mercy endures forever.

—Psalm 118:1

"I need to pray more!" All Christians say this at one time or another; some of us say it almost every day. It is a holy desire. We want to know the Lord and spend time with him. However, spending *more* time with him may not be easy. In our modern, technological world, we often feel busy and stressed. We want to pray—but when and how?

What if you could grow closer to God by using a special prayer that takes just ten minutes each day? St. Ignatius shows us a way to do exactly that. It's something that he did himself. In fact, he told the early Jesuits that no matter what—no matter how busy they get with preaching and teaching—they should never omit this prayer. It's called the "Examination of Conscience," or simply, the Examen. One Jesuit author even renamed it the "Consciousness Examen."[4] Whatever you want to call it, this prayer is a way of looking back on your day and thanking God for the blessings that he has given you. When you hear the phrase "Examination of Conscience" you may associate this with preparation for Confession. Yes, it can be used for that purpose. Ignatius outlines a practice called the Particular Examen in the *Spiritual Exercises* specifically for those getting ready for the Sacrament of Reconciliation. However, in this exercise, we'll be praying the General Examen; Ignatius recommends this as a daily practice to help us become more fully aware of God's action and our own response (see 24–44 in the *Exercises* for Ignatius's full description of both examens).

Recall the gospel passage from the introduction of this book. Jesus sends the disciples out for ministry and then "the apostles gathered together with Jesus and reported all they had done and taught. He said to them, 'Come away by yourselves to a deserted place and rest a while'" (Mk 6:30–31). The disciples, including all of us, need to talk with Jesus about the events in our daily lives. Jesus can help us to understand our experiences, and how the Holy Spirit was at work in us in each one. With Christ, we can also humbly acknowledge our own weaknesses and shortcomings. Each day, the Examen helps us to talk informally with Christ about our day. At the most basic level, the Examen is this: Jesus looks at each of us with love and asks, "How was your day?" Christ calls us into communion, and sharing our lives with him each day helps us to experience this communion. My life is better when I do this regularly. Instead of rushing from one event to the next, I stop a few times during the day to consider what has happened so far. I take a deep breath, reflect, and thank God for a few blessings in my day.

The Examen is based on a few basic truths: God is good and he loves you (recall how we explored this in the first exercise). God listens to you and helps you. With his grace and a bit of effort, you can notice God's action and then thank him. (Recall the second exercise.) This is awareness. God is active in your life every day at every moment. (Recall your Top 10 from the third exercise.) This daily practice will help you to deepen your relationship with him.

The Examen is a simple form of prayer directed toward developing a spiritual sensitivity to the special ways God approaches you, invites you, and calls you each day. This prayer helps you to keep your heart centered on Christ throughout the day, and it can be done in the evening or midday. It takes five to fifteen minutes, and the more frequently you do it the more natural it becomes, offering a daily way of consciousness, a way of growing in your relationship with God. Here it is in five easy steps:

STEP 1: BEGIN

- Intro: Sit or kneel. Read a brief prayer or scripture passage.
- Enter God's presence.

STEP 2: GIVE THANKS

- Pray, "Lord, help me to look on this day with gratitude."
- Reflect on the day: events, people, conversations, emotions.
- Identify three specific moments that you are grateful for.

STEP 3: NAME THE SORROWS AND SINS

- Notice your sorrow and sins. Be specific. Hold them up to his light.

STEP 4: PETITION

- Ask for God's blessings on self, project, family, and so on.

STEP 5: LOOK AHEAD TO THE NEXT TWENTY-FOUR HOURS AND CONCLUDE

- Ask for trust and hope. What are God's hopes for you?
- Close with a Hail Mary or another familiar prayer.

OVERVIEW: THE EXAMEN AND YOU

The Examen is the ultimate prayer for busy people; you don't
need a Bible or a prayer book to do it. All you need is your mind,
your heart, and a few minutes with the Lord. A few years ago, I
worked in campus ministry at Rockhurst High School in Kansas
City, Missouri. It was a fun and crazy assignment. Rockhurst is
a classic Jesuit all-boys high school, and in addition to teaching, I helped organize retreats, Masses, and prayer services for
one thousand teenage boys. I called bus companies, updated
spreadsheets, and met with teachers and students. I ran in and
out of classrooms, hallways, and conference rooms all day. Boys
popped into my office every day with permission slips, excuses,
and questions:

"Can I switch to the October retreat?"

"I can't serve at Mass on Friday because I have a lacrosse
game."

"Fr. Laramie, could God microwave a burrito so hot that
he himself could not eat it?" (I think that question came from
a *Simpsons* episode!)

You get the idea.

Although my job was to help the boys to pray, it was often
hard for *me* to find time to pray during the school day. The one
prayer I consistently prayed at school was the Examen during
my forty-five-minute lunch break. The bell rang at 12:10, and I
went to the cafeteria, ate a bite, chatted with a few teachers, and
then walked to the chapel for my Examen. I had, at most, ten

minutes in the chapel; at 12:55 the bell rang again and I'd have another project, another event, or another phone call.

For me, the Examen offered a moment of peace. It was a chance to look over my day, thank the Lord, and prayerfully look ahead to the next event or activity. I always walked out of that chapel feeling refreshed. Days that I skipped the Examen were always more stressful and more chaotic. In fact, when I missed my Examen I always got *less* done because I was *more* stressed out. Some days I'd think, *Today is so crazy that I can't do my Examen.* Over time, the Lord changed my perspective, so that I started to think, *Today is so crazy that I can't* skip *my Examen.* Ten minutes with the Lord each day made my life more peaceful and more fruitful. Let's look at the five steps, fleshed out.

STEP 1: BEGIN

We begin by beginning. For step one, Catholics may want to start with a Hail Mary, an Our Father, or another familiar prayer. This gets the "spiritual juices" flowing for the Examen. It can help us if we also perform a physical action: make the Sign of the Cross, genuflect, kneel before a cross, or sit in a peaceful place. Some people jokingly call these actions "Catholic calisthenics"; in church, we bow, kneel, and touch holy water. Physical actions help us to engage the body, mind, and spirit in prayer. These ancient practices are highly practical; they help us to begin our prayer with our attention on the Lord.

This step is the most important of the five steps. Why? Because this step begins our prayer! The Examen doesn't work if we don't do it. Have you ever made a great New Year's resolution? Perhaps you said, "I want to eat more kale, eat less red meat, and walk a mile every day." But then, January 1 became January 31 and you never actually did anything. A short, concrete beginning is the best way to start the Examen. "In the name of the Father, and of the Son, and of the Holy Spirit . . ."

STEP 2: GIVE THANKS

Step two is a brief overview of the last twenty-four hours. I "give thanks to God our Lord for the benefits that I have received," writes Ignatius (*SE*, 43). I thank him for all he has given me this day. What happened today? For most of us, *a lot* happens in twenty-four hours: meetings or classes, phone calls, errands, conversations, and perhaps dinner with family. You don't need to recall every single activity. Rather, take a moment to reflect leisurely on the past day. You might recall the Top 10 exercise in exercise 3: What stands out? What were the joyful moments? Where was Christ at work in your life? You may think of a smile from a child, a nice lunch, a brisk breeze as you walked to the car, a meeting that went well. Ask Christ to show you how he was at work in your day. Thank him. Be specific. Cultivating gratitude means thanking God for real, concrete things and events.

STEP 3: NAME THE SORROWS AND SINS

In this step, name the sorrows and sins of your day. We all deal with anxiety, illness, traffic jams, and arguments at some point in our lives. This is an opportunity to bring these situations and events to the Lord and hold them up to his light. Think of a stained-glass window in a church: in the dark, you simply see a grey and murky window. When light shines through, images emerge, showing a vivid, colorful scene. Sin is real, suffering is real, and Christ can work through our sins and sufferings if we let him.

For example, perhaps you had a tense conversation with a coworker this morning, and you still feel upset about it. As you hold this event up to Christ's light, maybe you get a sense of your coworker's stress and tiredness. He seemed really critical toward you; as you pray about him, you remember that he's been helping a sick relative for several weeks. You may also see that you were mostly charitable with him, even though he was not very friendly toward you. Notice how this scene changes as you bring it to prayer in the Examen. Instead of just a bad encounter with a grumpy person, you engage the Lord in a holy conversation; you thank him for the gift of patience and then pray for this troubled man.

In step three, you should "ask grace to know my sins and rid myself of them" (*SE*, 43); this includes your thoughts, words, and actions. We'll take more time to look specifically at our personal sins in later exercises. In the daily Examen, you want to become aware of your own activities and take responsibility for them. The fruit of the Examen is a heart that is more sensitive, more reflective, and more loving—as opposed to a heart that is cold, calloused, and unaware. The Lord promises us, "I will give you a new heart, and a new spirit I will put within you. I will remove the heart of stone from your flesh and give you a heart of flesh" (Ez 36:26). It can be painful and even embarrassing to notice your sins and faults, even small ones. You can also notice patterns; perhaps you tend to be an angry, unsafe driver when you are in a hurry. The remedy may be simply leaving a bit earlier. By bringing your bad habits to the Lord in prayer, you can experience his forgiveness and healing. Over time, the Examen helps you to grow and improve in these areas of your life. The fruit of the Examen is an increase in gratitude. With his grace and our effort, we sin less and love more.

STEP 4: PETITION

Now you ask the Lord to bless your actions and your family members. You can even petition him to help you in your struggles. Indeed, we now begin to see the very logical flow of this prayer, this Examen. We start with gratitude, name our sorrows, and then ask Christ for blessings upon all these different parts of our lives.

Step 4 is often a quick "Examen of my Examen." You recall the joys and sorrows of the day that you have just named; you then consciously lift these people and events up to the Lord. Prayers of petition touch upon one of the mysteries of Christian life: God is all good and all powerful. We are limited, but God loves us. He works through you and me. We can accept his love and guidance or we can reject it. We need his help to cooperate with his will.

From experience, I can tell you that it feels good to do God's will. It's not always easy. But when I am walking with Jesus in daily life, I feel a quiet peace and joy. It feels right.

STEP 5: LOOK AHEAD TO THE NEXT TWENTY-FOUR HOURS AND CONCLUDE

Finally, in step five you look ahead to the next twenty-four hours. What events will likely occur in the day ahead? Maybe you have an important meeting scheduled. Or you're driving a carpool, or coaching a soccer practice, going for a run, making dinner—or all of the above. Who will you see? How will God be at work? What are you looking forward to? What are you excited about, nervous about, worried about? Look ahead and briefly place all of these situations in God's hands. He's in charge. You simply need to do your part and receive his grace. It may not all be easy, but you can trust in his wisdom and love. Then close with a familiar prayer—perhaps an Our Father, a Hail Mary, or a quick line from scripture, such as "The LORD is my shepherd; there is nothing I lack" (Ps 23:1).

We all hunger to find meaning and purpose in our lives. The Examen is a prayer that builds on these natural desires. In the Examen, I ask God to help me understand my life story as it unfolds each day. What is an evening news show but a recap of the day's events? What is ESPN's *SportsCenter* but a look at the highlights and lowlights of the day in sports—an athletic examen? For married couples, a familiar greeting each evening is, "Hi, Honey; how was your day?" It's almost as if your spouse said, "Honey, share with me your examination of conscience according to St. Ignatius of Loyola." Businesses compile quarterly reports to examine performances, successes, and weaknesses. We do different kinds of examens all of the time. However, it is essential that we deliberately bring the Lord into this conversation, to ask God, "How have you been at work in my day? How have you blessed me and challenged me? How can I cooperate more fully in the P&F—which is your great plan for me?"

JESUS ASKS, "HOW WAS YOUR DAY?"

The Examen may feel clumsy at first, but this practice gets easier the more we do it, just like dancing a waltz, riding a bike, or using chopsticks. It takes a few tries to get the hang of it. You may not get through all five steps in ten minutes. That is okay. Hang in there. Keep trying.

I do not pray it perfectly. However, I can say that the Examen is my favorite prayer, and it is the most important prayer that I pray each day. The Examen helps me to see Christ's action in my daily life; the Lord works in small ways every day. In Luke's gospel, two disciples cry out with joy, "Were not our hearts burning [within us] while he spoke to us on the way . . . ?" (24:32). Jesus speaks and acts in my life each day; the Examen helps me to notice him, listen to him, and respond with gratitude.

Sometimes it can feel like your spiritual life is separate from your daily life. On one side, you can have prayer, scripture, and perhaps Mass, other religious services, and retreats. On the other side, you can have school, a job, family duties, email, music, TV, shopping, and sports. Our modern technological culture only exacerbates the division. The Examen helps to bridge this separation. For Jesus and the saints, life is an integrated whole; the Holy Spirit guides and blesses us in our daily routines, during our sufferings, in prayer, in work, and beyond. Through the Examen, the Spirit makes us whole and integrates our lives in Christ.

QUESTIONS AND ACTIVITIES

1. Set up a reminder for yourself to pray the Examen for the next several days. For example, you may want to use your phone to take a photo of the five steps; then you can pray it even if you don't have this book with you. Or you could copy down the five steps on a slip of paper and post this on your bathroom mirror. Or schedule a fifteen-minute window of time in your personal calendar.

2. Read Psalm 23. Ask the Lord to show you how he is with you in "green pastures" as well as in "the valley of the shadow of death."

3. Pray the Examen now, using the five steps. It should take about ten to fifteen minutes.

4. After you pray the Examen, jot down a few notes—especially three specific people/events that you are grateful for today.

5. Pray the Examen once this week with someone you care about. This could be a spouse, friend, grandchild, or someone in your prayer group. You could briefly explain the steps, take a few minutes in quiet prayer, and then share with your friend a few of the graces of your day.

A Blessed Heart: Gratitude for My Gifts and Talents

A body is one though it has many parts.

—1 Corinthians 12:12

"What are you good at?" This is a question that grade school kids exchange on the playground each day, usually related to the sports game at hand. "I'm good at soccer, he's better at basketball, but she's faster than all of us!" As we get older, we have opportunities to develop a wide variety of interests—carpentry, accounting, singing, or baking.

"What are you good at *spiritually*?" This might be a question we have not thought much about. Many of us might be quicker to point out our faults and weaknesses rather than our spiritual strengths and gifts. In the *Spiritual Exercises*, St. Ignatius encourages us to "call back into our memory the gifts that we have received—our creation, redemption, and other gifts particular to ourselves. We will ponder with deep affection how much God our Lord has done for us, and how much he has given us of what he possesses" (*SE*, 234). In the preceding exercises, we've spent some time considering God's gifts of creation, redemption, and love for humanity—these gifts are offered to all people. Now let's take some time to reflect on the spiritual gifts unique to you and me as individuals.

To help us examine our own gifts, let's look at a few saints and their unique spiritual gifts. We will notice that different saints excelled in different areas of the spiritual life. We have heroic missionaries such as St. Isaac Jogues, S.J.; he was one of the North American martyrs who brought the Christian faith to native peoples in Canada and the northeast United States in the 1600s. We recall brilliant writers such as St. Augustine, who dove deeply into the mysteries of Christ's life through poetry, homilies, and books. Think of mystics such as St. Thérèse of Lisieux; she spent long hours in prayer and contemplation with Christ.

How about you? What are you good at spiritually? You and I may feel intimidated by these spiritual giants, but they can be great models for us because they help us to realize that God works through our spiritual talents and abilities.

WHO, ME?

For young Jesuits, the formation program is designed to push them beyond their comfort zones. They are asked to study philosophy and foreign languages and to work in unfamiliar settings. During my formation, I helped lead a retreat in a women's prison in California, and I baptized Mayan children in an isolated village in Central America. Through these experiences, the Lord helped me to develop my spiritual gifts and to discover a few others that I didn't know I had. Parenting and family life can also put people in situations that are awkward, challenging, and sometimes ridiculous: balancing the family checkbook; changing a diaper for the first time; winning an argument with a five-year-old:

"No, I didn't."

"Yes, you did."

"*No*, I didn't."

In the process, you rely on the Lord, recognize your strengths, and discover a few gifts that you didn't know you had.

In my Jesuit formation, I've grown in my knowledge of Christ and human nature. I've had some great teachers, and I've read some excellent books about scripture and theology. I've also slowly grown in wisdom. By working as a spiritual director, I've gotten better at really listening to others and only then offering them some feedback or advice. No one wants a know-it-all priest. First, I've got to get to know the other person and understand her situation. Only then can I get a sense of how

God is working in her life. From there we can discuss the next step regarding her prayer or a big decision.

So what are you good at spiritually? Many of us are quick to dodge this question. "Who, me? Oh, I'm not very good at spiritual stuff. I just try to say my prayers and be nice to people. I've never had visions, or written spiritual poetry, or things like that." But, let's recall our earlier exercise where we reflected on the book of Genesis: "God said: Let us make human beings in our image, after our likeness," and "he found [us] very good" (1:26, 31). This applies to each one of us. Many of us have been studying, praying, and living our faith for many years. In my own experience, I have found that Christians today tend to overlook or ignore their spiritual gifts. They may do this in a misguided attempt at humility—we're not supposed to brag, right? However, if we downplay our abilities, then we risk minimizing or wasting the gifts that God has given to us. And he does not want us to waste his gifts!

The Church offers us several lists of spiritual gifts in St. Paul's letters, in the Old Testament, and in the *Catechism of the Catholic Church*. Among the lists of spiritual gifts are the seven fruits of the Holy Spirit, twelve gifts of the Holy Spirit, seven Catholic virtues, and eight beatitudes. No one has all of these gifts, except Jesus; in fact, all of these gifts flow from his Sacred Heart to enrich the Church and the world. Each of us, however, has received some combination of these spiritual gifts, and Jesus wants us to use them. These gifts are *meant* to be used. Jesus tells us not to "light a lamp and then put it under a bushel basket" but rather to set it "on a lampstand, where it gives light to all in the house" (Mt 5:15). Paul reminds us that these gifts are given to us "for building up the church" (1 Cor 14:12). It's true; not every one of us is a mystic, but God does not want every person to be a mystic! St. Paul tells us that "a body is one though it has many parts" (1 Cor 12:12). If we all use our spiritual gifts to the best of our ability, together we strengthen the Body of Christ.

Look at your life and into your heart: Which gifts do you have? Which gifts would you like to have? Look over the lists below. We'll reflect on a few of these spiritual gifts in the next few pages.

GIFTS, FRUITS, AND VIRTUES

- *Seven gifts of the Holy Spirit.* See Isaiah 11, *Catechism* 1830–1845.

  » wisdom, understanding, counsel, knowledge, fortitude, piety, and fear of the Lord (wonder/awe)

- *Twelve fruits of the Holy Spirit.* See Galatians 5:22 and *Catechism* 1830–1846.

  » charity, joy, peace, patience, kindness, goodness, generosity, gentleness, faithfulness, modesty, self-control, and chastity

- *Seven Catholic virtues.* See 1 Corinthians 13:13 and *Catechism* 1803–1829.

  » cardinal virtues: prudence, justice, temperance, courage/fortitude

  » theological virtues: faith, hope, charity/love

- *Eight Beatitudes.* See Matthew 5:3–12.

  » Blessed are . . . the poor in spirit, those who mourn, the meek, those who hunger and thirst for righteousness, the merciful, the pure of heart, the peacemakers, those persecuted for righteousness, those persecuted for Jesus

- *Supernatural gifts.* See various books of the New Testament.

  » miracles, healing, tongues, interpretation of tongues, word of wisdom/knowledge, prophecy, reading souls, ability to strengthen faith in others

- Natural gifts of leadership/service. See St. Paul's letters for fuller descriptions.

  » discernment of spirits, teaching, preaching, missionary work, prophecy (for poor, unborn, etc.), helping/serving (poor, elderly, etc.), and leadership (bishop, priest, deacon, and other Church leadership roles)

SEVEN GIFTS OF THE HOLY SPIRIT

Let's begin with the seven gifts of the Holy Spirit. Many of us studied these gifts as teenagers when we were preparing for the

Sacrament of Confirmation. We won't discuss every single gift on the list; I'll give an overview of a few gifts to give you a basic idea. You can then look at your own life to see how God has blessed you. What is the special combination of gifts that God has uniquely given to you?

If you are a teacher or a parent, God has probably given you the gifts of wisdom and understanding. These gifts help you to listen to your students or children, guide them on a good path, and know how to help them with their problems. Some of you may be thinking, "Those aren't really spiritual gifts. That's just good parenting." Wisdom and understanding are spiritual gifts that God gives us for very practical purposes. St. Paul tells us that God gives us gifts "to equip the holy ones for the work of ministry, for building up the body of Christ" (Eph 4:12). For Christians, parenting is not just a role. It is a vocation from the Lord. God creates children through the love of a man and woman. Christ calls parents and teachers to love, help, and guide children by raising them; he gives the gifts of wisdom and understanding to help us live our vocation and build up the Body of Christ, the Church.

As a former teacher, I know that it is not easy to be patient and understanding with young people. It demands prayer, reflection, and practice. In my first few years, I frequently consulted older teachers. They knew how to educate and form teenagers. This is where grandparents play an important role; they can share their experience to aid the next generation of parents.

Nurses and engineers alike draw upon the gifts of wisdom and understanding in their daily routines. They both must diagnose a situation and then apply an appropriate remedy. A patient with an upset stomach may have simple indigestion or a serious intestinal infection. The nurse must consider the patient's other symptoms, his or her family history, and other medical issues. An engineer who is designing a bridge over a large canyon must measure the expanse, test the soil for its durability, consider the number of cars that will drive on the road, and so on. Wisdom and understanding are two gifts that must work closely together. A caring psychologist or confessor must carefully listen to the other person with respect and compassion. What is really going on? What does this client or penitent really need to overcome the problem? Only after careful listening can the counselor give helpful advice.

Let's consider the gift of fortitude. The *Catechism* tells us that "*fortitude* is the moral virtue that ensures firmness in difficulties and constancy in the pursuit of the good. It strengthens the resolve to resist temptations and to overcome obstacles in the moral life" (1808). Fortitude is something like "grit"—it means that we don't give up when the going gets tough. It's not always easy to be a disciple of Christ, or a parent, or a teacher, or a priest. When life is difficult, and suffering is real, do you give up? Do you back down from Christ's call? Or do you turn to the Lord in prayer? Can you ask others for support? Are you willing to redouble your efforts and try again? I recall my first year of teaching at an all-boys high school. I taught public speaking. I tried lecturing for most of the class; after a few minutes they would zone out and chitchat with one another. I switched gears and tried group projects; this worked for a while, and then quickly devolved into chaos. A few times the students were so loud that the principal would stop in to ask, "Everything okay?" They'd quiet down until he left. One day, I brought them to the cafeteria to spread out and practice their speeches; in the midst of this, a boy somehow managed to set the microwave on fire. (That's another story.) It took several long weeks for me to find a mix of lecture, small group work, and presentations that kept the class (more or less) engaged and on task. Fortitude is not an easy virtue. It's a hard road, but it may be the only way up the mountain.

TWELVE FRUITS OF THE HOLY SPIRIT

Have you ever looked up at a constellation in the night sky? You can draw an invisible line between several stars to form the Big Dipper or Orion's Belt. Similarly, several of these twelve gifts of the Holy Spirit can be viewed as a sort of spiritual constellation: charity, joy, peace, patience, kindness, goodness, generosity, and gentleness are all closely connected. Seeing this list, you might immediately think of someone you know who fits this description—perhaps a loving grandfather, a religious sister from your youth, or a faithful friend. The gifts of charity, joy, peace, patience, and kindness are sometimes called "soft virtues." They are relational; they help us deepen our relationship with God and others. They lend a warmth and sweetness to

Christian life. Other spiritual gifts, such as fortitude, wisdom, and knowledge, are "hard virtues." They give a structure and definition to life; people with these gifts are often leaders in Church, business, and culture. They are like strong bones that support the Body of Christ. The soft virtues are like the muscles and flesh that overlay the bones; these gifts are beautiful, inviting, and available to everyone—including the poor, the weak, and those with minimal education. Yet sometimes the soft virtues are most important in the powerful. We see this in Jesus himself, the all-powerful, divine Son of God. With infinite wisdom and knowledge, he softly and gently reaches out to children, the sick, and the elderly. The virtues of patience and charity help to cultivate communion with Christ and others. Which gifts has God blessed you with? Which gifts might you need to grow in most?

NATURAL AND SUPERNATURAL GIFTS

We begin to see some overlap in these different lists. Charity and peace show up more than once. So do justice and knowledge. Important themes recur in scripture with slight variations in tone. God repeats certain sayings in different ways to help us ponder specific truths and apply them to our lives.

Natural and supernatural gifts likewise work together and complement one another. In the gospels, we see that Jesus has miraculous gifts of insight and healing. Some saints also had these abilities. St. Peter heals a paralyzed man and even raises the dead after Jesus' Resurrection (Acts 3:1–8, 9:36–41). In the

1900s, St. Padre Pio is said to have had the ability to read souls; this means that he could sense a person's inner joys and failings before they even spoke to him. These are supernatural gifts; they are rare. But they do occur. In the history of the Church, some priests and mystics have received these gifts. The Anointing of the Sick is a prayerful sacrament through which we ask God for healing; first, the minister asks for spiritual healing, and second, the minister asks for bodily healing. In more everyday forms of healing, physicians and nurses have a responsibility to heal the sick.

The natural gifts on the list are actually clusters of other, smaller human gifts.

We may say, "She's a great leader." What do we mean? We probably mean that she is an effective public speaker, she is a good listener, she is able to take bold and decisive action, she is not afraid of being unpopular, and so on. What about good teachers? They are often creative, thoughtful, intelligent, caring, organized, and passionate.

All of the gifts on these lists, big and small, are given by God to be used. They are meant to build up the Body of Christ, the Church. They can be used in powerful and dramatic ways—as we see in heroic martyrs such as St. Isaac Jogues, S.J., or loving servants such as St. Teresa of Calcutta. For others, God calls us to use these gifts in humble daily gestures. For some of us, this means praying, studying, feeding our children, and caring for sick relatives; we rely on the spiritual gifts of fortitude and joy, peace and patience.

No matter if you're in high school, retirement, or somewhere in between, you may be discerning God's call for your next steps: Should you go to college, make a career change, relocate closer to family? Your spiritual gifts may give you a hint as to where God is leading you and what he has in store for you. We can also ask God for additional gifts; he may say yes, or he may say no (in which case he is asking you to use the gifts he has already given you!).

QUESTIONS AND ACTIVITIES

1. Look over each of these lists. Ask the Lord to help you recognize which gifts he has given you. Then, from each section, write down one virtue that you possess. Beware of self-doubt! God has certainly blessed you with some of these gifts. For example, you might write: "I have wisdom, patience, courage, and faith. I am merciful, I help increase faith in others, and I can teach." Thank God for each of these gifts.

2. Look at the gifts you wrote down. Think about one specific time that you used each of these gifts effectively. Then write a brief description for each. For example: "wisdom— I gave Emily some good advice last week when she talked to me about her problems with her older sister."

3. Focus on one gift on your list. Think of one holy person who also has this gift (a person in the Bible, a saint or another historical figure, or a friend or relative). Learn more about

this person's life and his or her gift (which you have, too!). You might do this by using the Bible, talking to him or her (face-to-face or in prayer), or by researching his or her life.

4. In the coming days, notice how these gifts/fruits come up in your daily Examen. Do you notice yourself using one or more of these gifts consistently? Wisdom? Charity? Is there a gift that you frequently need? Patience? Gentleness? Thank the Lord for his gifts to you, and ask him for what you still need.

5. Many of us wish we had more joy and peace in our daily lives. How many of us have prayed for these gifts? Further, we may want to talk with someone who appears joyful and peaceful. How do they do it? How do they share joy and cultivate peace in a wounded world? How did Jesus do it during his time of ministry?

EXERCISE 7

A Divided Heart: Vices, Storms, and Temptations

I am the LORD your God,

who brought you out of the land of

Egypt, out of the house of slavery.

—Exodus 20:2

In the last exercise, we reflected on our gifts and blessings. For many of us, this is an enjoyable activity: it is natural to rejoice in the good things that God has given to us. We want to use these gifts more fully to serve the Lord and others with our whole hearts. Sometimes, however, we might be reluctant to acknowledge and use our gifts. This could be due to a poor self-image, lack of self-knowledge, or painful experiences from our past. We'll address some of these issues in this exercise and in exercises eight and nine.

It's even less fun to ponder the gifts you lack. Who wants to wonder what they're bad at? Maybe you feel some dread just reading that question, thinking, *What am I bad at? Ugh. Lots of stuff.* And understandably, our failures aren't something we want to share with people in our lives. On social media platforms such as Facebook, Twitter, and Instagram, we tend to share our accomplishments and victories with friends:

"My team won the softball game!"

"My son is an honor student!"

"Look at how I remodeled our kitchen!"

Maybe we trumpet these positives in an attempt to hide our negative qualities. But in Christian life, we need to have a realistic sense of our strengths *and* weaknesses. What are some of your challenges, weaknesses, and temptations? Once you are aware of these, you can offer them to the Lord, and then ask him to help you grow in these areas; with his grace, you can mature as his disciple.

A SPIRITUAL FORTRESS

St. Ignatius uses his experience on a battlefield to help us understand our spiritual weaknesses. He says that the devil is like "a military commander who is attempting to conquer and plunder his objective. . . . [He] studies the strengths and weaknesses of a fortress, and then attacks at its weakest point. In the same way, the enemy of human nature prowls around and from every side and probes all our theological, cardinal and moral virtues. Then at the point where he finds us weakest and most in need in regard to our eternal salvation, there he attacks and tries to take us" (*SE*, 327). Imagine yourself in a fortress, a structure with high walls, thick gates, and perhaps even a moat and draw-bridge. Recall the virtues and gifts from the previous exercise: faith, hope, and love; prudence, justice, courage, etc. Honestly ask the Lord, "What are my weak points?" For example, maybe you've had problems with your bosses in your last three jobs, leading you to quit all three. Did you really have three bad bosses? Or could it be that you have unrealistic expectations? Are you sufficiently prudent and temperate? Do you get along well with others, or are you constantly in conflict with your coworkers?

In a strange way, the devil might be doing us a favor by exposing the weaknesses in our fortresses. When we see these problematic patterns in our lives, we can turn to the Lord and ask for help. With him, we can try to change for the better.

Instead of a fortress, let's use another concrete image: a house. Imagine that a major thunderstorm pounds your town with pouring rain and gale-force winds. The clouds clear and you look over the damage to your house. Your back door is unhinged because it was not properly secured. Your basement leaks along one wall because the builder forgot to seal the cement joint. Perhaps you were unaware of these issues before the storm. As a wise homeowner, what do you do? Do you say, "Gosh, I hope we don't have any more big storms this year!" Or do you dutifully repair the damage and go further still and rein-force those fragile areas of your home? If you are prudent, you'll be ready for next storm so it does not bring further destruction. You'll add strong bolts to the back door's hinges. You will also be smart enough to ask for help; you'll bring in a professional to seal the leaky spot in the foundation.

Try to bring this concept into your spiritual life after you experience a period of stress or suffering. Where is your spiritual house solid and secure? Where does it need repair and reinforcement? Jesus spoke of the "the wise man who built his house on rock" (Mt 7:24), urging his followers to establish a firm foundation for their spiritual lives.

AFTER THE STORM

I've been through plenty of storms myself. A stressful week, an argument with a coworker, a Mass where everything seems to go wrong: "Wait, the microphone doesn't work and we're out of wine?!" The storm is not fun, but storms are part of life. Jesus himself had difficult encounters with his disciples and the crowds. Can we learn from the storms? Can we grow from them? If not, then a storm is just an experience of suffering with no real redemption. After the storm, we need to bring our pain to Jesus and maybe get help from another person as well. It's humbling to ask for help, but in conversation with Christ, we can assess the situation and start again. Fix the door, patch the leak, and be better prepared. The devil will probably attack that same spot again. With Jesus, you can be stronger and smarter next time.

Storms reveal our weaknesses. Perhaps you feel stressed out from a tough week at work. Maybe you said yes to too many projects because you were afraid of disappointing others. This led you to work extra-long hours and minimize your sleep. When the weekend arrives, you're still tired and frustrated, and you take it out on your family. You may think the storm that damaged your spiritual house is your job; however, the storm may really be your fear of failure at work. Praying the Examen regularly can help you to notice your own patterns of behavior and keep track of the emotions in your heart. If you realize you are tired and grumpy with your family every Saturday, then you need to address this. Before you agree to a heavy week of work assignments, think of the impact this will have on your family. Perhaps you can even embrace the virtue of humility and discuss the situation with your boss or colleagues: explain that you're eager to work hard, but your commitment to your family limits the late nights you can give to the job. St. Paul tells us that "all things work for good for those who love God" (Rom 8:28). With Christ, we can learn and grow from our faults and failings. In humility, we recognize our weaknesses following a spiritual storm.

Let's apply this image more broadly to our own spiritual lives. Some of our shortcomings may be obvious, such as sleeping late instead of attending church on Sunday with the rest of the family. Maybe a young man has been dealing with a drinking problem for several years. He tries to improve—well, sort of tries. But he quickly slides back into this habit. His friends all know. Everyone sees how this negatively affects his family, work, and religious practice. They say, "James is a great guy; if only he could kick that habit."

Other weaknesses might be more hidden. Perhaps you tend to be very impatient and do not listen carefully to others. The sin of pride might be the root cause, making you dismiss other people and not value their experiences. Many of us maintain a vague awareness of our sins and bad habits; they make us uncomfortable, so we try to ignore them. But if we lean into this discomfort, we can learn more about ourselves and make changes for the better. Are you often gossiping about enemies, friends, and relatives? What's really going on here? Consider that perhaps you're jealous of their gifts or opportunities; maybe you feel that your gifts are insignificant compared to theirs. Have you brought this struggle to Jesus? Does he think your gifts are insignificant? Probably not. In fact, definitely not.

As we look honestly at our flaws and limitations, the goal is not misery and shame. We seek a clear-eyed humility. We recall that God made us and loves us. We want to speak to the Lord honestly and ask for his help and support. Of course, Christ already knows your weaknesses! (Your close friends probably do, too!) With his help, you can acknowledge them and bring them into his light. In some cases, you may need additional help to grow in these areas. Friends, mentors, spiritual directors, counselors, support groups, and twelve-step programs are just a few of the supports that God offers us. Certainly, prayer is the primary means of support. In addition, God often calls us to cooperate with his work as he strengthens us. The wise person realizes that he or she can't do everything all the time; the wise homeowner calls in a professional when a complicated problem arises on the property. Just so, the daily Examen can help us notice our weaknesses and bad habits; daily prayer can help us to turn to Christ, the Master Builder, for repair and healing.

CHRISTIAN WISDOM REGARDING SIN AND VICE

The Church gives us different lists to help us examine our hearts in many different areas. In the last exercise, we looked at lists of graces, virtues, and gifts. There are also corresponding lists of sins and vices. Specifically, here we'll look at the seven deadly sins and the sins the Ten Commandments warn against. The deadly sins have a long history in Christian tradition. Frequently they are not sins per se but rather selfish tendencies that we need to watch out for. For example, let's take the sin of pride. Perhaps you've been blessed with a good education; you have a successful job and important expertise in your field. These are all good things. However, you may need to be careful of your tendency toward arrogance, which leads you to treat others with a condescending attitude.

Many saints struggled with certain sins and vices. For Ignatius of Loyola, pride was an ongoing challenge. He was an intelligent, refined man from an influential family, and in his youth he was guilty of boasting, dueling, and carousing. He sought glory for himself, his family, and his nation. And yet through Christ, over time, Ignatius was able to transform his pride. Instead of seeking glory for himself, he worked for the greater glory of God—in Latin, *Ad majorem Dei gloriam.* He later made this the official Jesuit motto. For St. Augustine, the sin of lust was a problem in his early life; through prayer and study, he discovered the gift of Christian chastity and helped others to live this as well. The Ten Commandments are a timeless list of teachings the Lord gives to us. Where do you often stumble? Is it with the eighth commandment (don't lie)? Or perhaps with the sixth (don't commit adultery or lust)?

Below, I've listed the seven deadly sins and the Ten Commandments. Look over each list. Which ones apply uniquely to your life? Honestly ask, "Lord, what am I bad at?" In the next few pages, I'll explain several vices and sins on these lists and help us to reflect on ourselves. With the help of the Lord, we can come to him in humility and ask for help in overcoming these bad habits, weaknesses, and failings.

SINS AND COMMANDMENTS

- *Two Greatest Commandments of Jesus.* See Matthew 22:36–40.

  » "Love the Lord, your God, with all your heart, with all your soul, and with all your mind."

  » "Love your neighbor as yourself."

- *Seven Deadly Sins.* See 1 John 2:16.

  » wrath, greed, sloth, pride, lust, envy, and gluttony

- *Ten Commandments.* See Deuteronomy 5:6–21 and Exodus 20:2–17.

  » Worship no other gods but only God.

  » Do not take the name of the Lord in vain.

  » Remember to keep holy the Lord's Day.

  » Honor your father and your mother.

  » Do not kill.

  » Do not commit adultery.

  » Do not steal.

  » Do not bear false witness.

  » Do not covet your neighbor's wife.

  » Do not covet your neighbor's goods.

SLOTH: NOT THE TREE-DWELLING MAMMAL

The seven deadly sins have been the subject of numerous paintings, films, and songs over the years. The deadly sins are basically selfish, unloving actions. Thankfully, not many of us exhibit all seven—most of us tend toward one or two. Let's take a moment to consider one of these: sloth.

Sloth is a type of laziness. It means that you choose frivolity and entertainment instead of doing the work that God calls you to. We all need downtime and vacations, of course. Jesus and the disciples followed the Jewish tradition of resting on the Sabbath, Saturday. But we usually know the difference between legitimate rest and shirking our duties. Consider a young man in college. He is bright and enrolled in a prestigious pre-med program. He has tests and papers in his classes every few weeks. Perhaps he finds himself pulling all-nighters a few times each month to cram for his exams. Why? Instead of studying a bit every day, he wastes lots of time playing video games and watching ESPN (hmm; sounds like my freshman year!). Is this a sin? It's certainly a self-defeating tendency. If he keeps it up, he risks squandering a great academic opportunity—and that is sinful. Maybe this young man does not appear to be slothful—he exercises, goes out with friends, maybe even volunteers to serve the poor. However, even though he is "busy about many things," he is not doing "the one thing necessary" (see Jesus with Martha and Mary in Luke 10:38–42).

ENVY: I WANT WHAT YOU HAVE

Envy shows up in both the list of deadly sins and the commandments (ninth and tenth). Envy is a basic dissatisfaction with the gifts God has given to us. It braids together both pride and despair into a knotty rope of covetousness. In many ways, our entire American consumer culture is built on the rotten foundation of envy. Advertisements try to stir up feelings of misery regarding our own lives; they try to draw us toward the sparkling glory of the newest phone, car, shampoo, vacation, or restaurant. They try to convince us that our exhaustion, loneliness, or plain sadness can be fixed with shiny new possessions or expensive experiences. Envy drags us down; we're constantly trying to snare what other people have, thinking, *Her husband is more successful than mine; he has a nicer house than I do; she's so funny and I'm so boring.* If we allow these tendencies to grow and fester, they can lead us in still worse directions. Instead of rejoicing in others' successes, we may try to destroy the good things others have received or begin endless ruminating on how unfair and unpleasant our lives are—so that we miss out on the blessings and the calling God has given to us.

As you look at your sins and weaknesses, it's important to remember that you're not powerless. God is with you. With his help, you can grow and change. It may not be easy, and it may not happen overnight, but you're already taking several important steps: you are making a retreat, you are looking honestly at your life, and you are speaking with the Lord in prayer. Ignatius encourages us to go against [in Latin, *agere contra*] our sinful desires and weaknesses (*SE*, 97). This means that we do the exact opposite of our sins. For example, if you have a bad habit of gossiping, then you make a serious effort to speak positively about others (and to remain silent if you can't be positive). *Agere contra* is a shrewd, empowering spiritual tactic. It's a way of showing God, yourself, and the evil spirit that you are not giving up. Christ is with you, he will help you, and you are going to work hard to strengthen your spiritual house.

QUESTIONS AND ACTIVITIES

1. It is not easy to look at our sins and weaknesses. Begin with a prayer of trust. Ask God to strengthen your faith and hope. Ask him to help you look honestly at your vices and temptations so that you can ask him for support and healing.

2. Look at the list of seven deadly sins. Which one do you struggle with the most? Perhaps you have noticed this in your daily Examen. What does this look like for you? Be specific. Jot down a brief example.

3. Look at the Ten Commandments. Which one do you struggle with the most? What does this look like for you? Be specific. Jot down a brief example.

4. Look at your responses to questions 2 and 3, above. Then, prayerfully talk with the Lord about this. Ask him to help you dig into the deeper root: What is the real cause here? Are you unhappy with your life and achievements? Are you afraid of being hurt by God or others?

5. Recall Ignatius's advice about *agere contra*, going against. What is one specific thing you can do to go against one of your sins or bad habits? Write this down. Try to do it once today. For example, if you tend toward despair, you could take time to look over your Top 10 list each day for the next month; this will help stir your sense of hope by recalling God's goodness to you.

6. Prayer, fasting, and penance are ancient Christian practices. These actions can help us to overcome our sinfulness. For the next twenty-four hours, choose one specific penance practice: you may want to abstain from meat or alcohol or you may want to pray the Sorrowful Mysteries of the Rosary.

Pause for Heart Check

You've completed seven Heart Exercises. Congratulations! You're more than halfway through your retreat! Let's pause again for another quick heart check. You could take a few minutes to do this now. Or you might choose to do this just before you begin exercise 8. Or if you have time, you could even take a full day to review the previous seven chapters, look through your notes, and thank God for the graces you have received. St. Ignatius tells us that review and repetition helps us in savoring in our hearts the graces we receive on retreat (*SE*, 2). You may want to jot down a few notes after reflecting on these questions:

1. How is your retreat going so far?

2. Are you taking time for daily prayer and journaling?

3. What has the Lord been doing in your heart during this retreat? (Are you experiencing peace, joy, etc.?)

4. What are a few key highlights of your retreat? Be specific.

5. Is there one section that you'd like to go back to—perhaps a scripture passage, a question, or an encounter with Jesus? You might take some time to pray with that section again.

6. Have you noticed any areas of ongoing resistance? Name this resistance and bring it to the Lord.

7. Are there any themes or patterns emerging in your prayer? What are they? (God's love, gratitude, etc.)

8. Have you noticed any big changes since your last heart check? What are they? (Prayer seems easier lately, or I'm feeling really distracted, etc.)

9. Are there any changes you need to make before you begin exercise 8?

A Wounded Heart: Patterns of Sin

A clean heart create for me, God;

renew within me a steadfast spirit.

—Psalm 51:12

I love the Christmas season because it's a time of joy and celebration filled with parties, friends, and beautiful liturgies. Christmas turns to New Year's Eve—another holiday of fun and food, song, and drink. A few days later, we all return to work and our usual routines. Eventually I peek at the calendar; I look at February and March, asking myself one question: When is Ash Wednesday? After the joys of Christmas and New Year's Eve, Ash Wednesday marks the beginning of the forty days of Lent. Lent is a season of sobriety, penance, and fasting. I may not like Lent, but I know I need it; Lent helps me to put my life in order.

We've now reached the Lenten moment of our retreat. That's right: it's time to talk about sin. Your sins. My sins. We've all got them. Thankfully, we can call upon Jesus, the "Lamb of God who takes away the sins of the world." Before we ask for forgiveness, we need to take a hard look at our lives. What sins have we committed? The writer G. K. Chesterton says that sin is the only Christian doctrine that can be proven by opening the daily newspaper. "War! Crime! Lust! Betrayal!" the headlines shout. It's all there. A sweep through human history shows us that sin has always been a problem in human society: whether two thousand years ago, one hundred years ago, or today. In fact, sin is *the* problem in the world. You're not the first person to sin, nor will you be the last. We're part of a long history of sin that is older than humankind. St. Ignatius briefly sketches a history of sin for us in the *Spiritual Exercises*. Getting a sense of the big picture of sin can help us come to grips with our own failings; then we can come to Christ and ask for forgiveness and help.

THE SIN OF ADAM AND EVE

In the *Spiritual Exercises*, Ignatius asks us to contemplate the first sin of the human race: that of Adam and Eve in Genesis 3. They were tempted to eat the forbidden fruit. They believed the serpent's lie instead of trusting in God's plan. The snake told them, "God knows well that when you eat of it your eyes will be opened and you will be like gods, who know" (v. 5). By eating the fruit, Adam and Eve were trying to become like God. Here's the irony—they were already like God! That's what it means to be made in God's image and likeness. We have the ability to know, to love, to be in relationship, and to be co-creators by procreation; furthermore, we share in God's power over creation through our dominion.

Ignatius points out that after the Fall, Adam and Eve "lived out their whole lives in great hardship and penance, deprived of the original justice which they had lost" (*SE*, 51). We see how they damaged their relationship with God and one another, suffered, and did penance for so long a time. With our imaginations, Ignatius invites us to deeply ponder this awful mystery. After everything God did for them, how did they respond? How often have we obeyed a slithering reptile instead of our glorious Creator? We bow to advertising, TV, sex, or selfishness instead of honoring the Lord who made us. We drown ourselves in shopping, pettiness, alcohol, or social media to avoid real relationships with God and our families. Imagine Adam and Eve's isolation, sorrow, and misery. We feel this, too. We, too, have tasted the long, ugly hangover that always results from sin: we all have felt sad, angry, guilty, and alone.

RESULTS OF SIN

Here's another angle on this meditation: reflect on one sin, carried to its logical conclusion. Most sins start small and grow bigger if we don't change our ways. For example, a married man sees that his wife is declining in health. She's tired, sick, weak, and unable to laugh and talk like she used to. He feels upset and alone. To avoid her suffering, he surfs the internet for hours and hours. Over time, he gravitates toward pornographic videos. Later, he flirts with a coworker and begins a romantic relationship. At first it's just coffee, then drinks, and then overnight visits. She gets pregnant. Panicked, he pressures her to have an abortion. He does all of this under a cloak of lies, denial, and secrecy. Again and again, the Lord pricks the man's conscience. Close friends notice his behavior and talk to him. "Michael, do you want to talk? Are you okay?" The man ignores these invitations. He puts up walls of denial. "It's not a big deal. It's none of your business. Do you realize what I've been through?" He's creating wreckage all around him. He has scarred his heart; it becomes hardened, almost petrified. He drifts from denial and egoism into despair. He never repents and never returns to God.

Meditating on sin may feel uncomfortable and harsh to many people today. We may ask, "What about God's mercy? Can't everyone receive forgiveness?" Of course God is merciful and everyone can receive forgiveness. But this does not negate the fact that our actions have consequences. If we choose a life of sin and selfishness, God will not force us to accept his grace. The Lord will call us back; he will encourage and challenge us through our family and friends, but God gives us freedom and honors our freedom. If you choose to live a sinful life, God will let you. The logical conclusion of a sinful life is hell because hell is eternal separation from God. Jesus speaks about hell more than once (see Matthew 13:42, 22:13). It is a tragic and real possibility for all of us. We choose heaven or hell through the choices we make each and every day.

WHAT ABOUT ME?

"What's wrong with the world today?" At bars and dining room tables, we hear heated discussions about this question. The answers are predictable: "Politicians! The media! Poverty and war, drugs and gangs!" G. K. Chesterton had a famous response to this question: "What's wrong with the world, sir? I am." It's so much easier to blame other people, other groups for the problems. But really, the answer is sin: that's what's wrong with the world. And Chesterton understands that we are all responsible for sin—we are all part of the problem. We need to start by taking responsibility for our own sinful thoughts, words, and deeds.

In this exercise, Ignatius asks us to pray for the grace of "shame and confusion" as we consider our own sins. You might be thinking, "Shame and confusion? Fr. Joe, I bought this book to get rid of my shame and confusion!" I understand, but shame, sorrow, and confusion are the proper responses to sin. Sin is illogical, unloving, stupid, and damaging. Why would we wreck God's beautiful plan? And yet we do it all the time, in small ways and big ways. Why do others distrust our Lord and reject his love? Why would we seek our own narrow, selfish will over God's loving plan for us? Sin is madness. And yet we do it all the time. Sin isn't something we can figure out, or solve. We must mourn it and ask the Lord for help to overcome our sins, to seek redemption.

PATTERNS OF SIN IN MY LIFE

Ignatius gives us a helpful framework for this exercise. He asks us to "call into memory all the sins of [your] life, looking at them year by year or period by period . . . first, the locality or house where [you] lived; second, the associations which [you] had with others; third, the occupation [you were] pursuing" (*SE*, 56). It helps to take a categorical approach to our sinfulness. What patterns do you notice? What were the main sins of your childhood, ages five to twelve? For many of us, these were playground scrapes, cursing, or petty theft. Who were your friends then? Did they encourage you to live a Christian life, or were they a bad influence? Were you a bad influence on them? Childhood sins are rarely serious, but they may lead you into uglier sins in your teenage years.

What about your junior high and high school years? Were you perhaps cheating on tests, drinking, using drugs, driving recklessly, or having premarital sex? What were the sins of your time in college or early adulthood: skipping church, lying to parents and teachers and bosses, or sleeping with a boyfriend or girlfriend? What about in your early married life? How about as a young parent or as a grandparent?

We probably notice certain patterns developing as we look back on these periods of life. You may see a habit of thrill seeking—first, by smoking cigarettes in junior high; later, in drunk driving and sexual flings. Or maybe laziness is a chronic problem for you—consistently shirking on homework or job, faith, and family responsibilities. We need to see our sins and bring them into Christ's light.

FROM DARKNESS INTO LIGHT

We all have a tendency to hide or ignore our sins. Who wants to post his or her sins on social media? Would you post "I stole another twenty-five dollars from my office today," or "I lied to my wife again so I could go to the bar"? Of course not. The tendency to hide or downplay our sins plays right into the hands of the evil spirit. The devil loves secrecy; he is always promising us, "No one will ever know!" Ignatius tells us that the devil is "like a false lover, insofar as he tries to remain secret and undetected. For such a scoundrel, speaking with evil intent and trying to seduce" us loves the cover of darkness (*SE*, 326). We hide behind our little white lies, as we stew in our guilt and embarrassment. Stop the denial. Name it for what it is: selfishness and betrayal toward God and others.

This is the solution that Ignatius proposes: share your temptations and sins with another person. Go tell your parents or your spouse or a close friend. A temptation is not a sin; in fact, it is possible that you've done nothing wrong. First, name the temptation. Then tell one trusted, faith-filled person. This can break the spell of Satan's powers. You don't need to post it on social media! Just tell one person you trust. Bring the temptation into the light of Christ. If you do fall into sin, then apologize to the person you've sinned against—the sooner the better. The Sacrament of Reconciliation employs a similar healthy course of action: making a confession to a priest also allows you to name your sins out loud. Ignatius writes, "When the person reveals them to his or her good confessor or some other spiritual person who understands the enemy's deceits . . . (the devil) quickly sees that he cannot succeed in the malicious project he began because his manifest deceptions have been detected" (*SE*, 326). Telling even one person helps you to break out of the vicious cycle of fear, doubt, sin, and evil. What if a fourteen-year-old boy had told his parents the first time he drank a beer with friends? Might this have spared him years of escalating drinking, alcoholism, and shame? What if the college student had said in Confession that she slept with someone after the party last Friday? Could this have prevented her long cycle of meaningless hookups?

If we try to fight the devil alone, we will lose. I know this from experience. I've had some excellent Jesuit superiors in my many assignments. And I've spoken with them quite honestly about my personal struggles and failings. This includes everything from living my vow of chastity to being a really bad Latin student. It is not easy to talk about these things. I prefer to ignore them or fight them alone; when I do, I always lose. Bringing these problems into the light brings me renewal and strength. Why fight alone and lose when you can fight together and win? Someone older and wiser than me can help to diagnose my problem so that I don't keep falling into the same traps. "Joe, what about a Latin tutor? Are you getting enough sleep?

What's the deeper issue that is affecting your relationships right now?"

Christian theology teaches us that Satan is a fallen archangel. He is smarter and stronger than I. But I am not alone! Look at Adam and Eve's fall in the garden. The devil tempted them to disobey God; Eve talked to the serpent. What if she had said, "Hey, Snake Eyes, I'm going to take a walk with my husband and talk this over. Better yet, Adam and I will bring this to God—who made us and loves us. Then we'll decide what to do." Talk to a trusted friend. Talk to a priest or pastor. Talk to Christ. Step out of the darkness and into his light.

SIN WRECKS COMMUNION

In our modern world, there are many confused notions regarding the true nature of sin. Comedians frequently make fun of religious teachings, celebrities revel in rebellion, and we say, "Woah, she's so cool! He's so powerful! She doesn't care what anyone thinks!" Sin is not just breaking a meaningless rule; sin wrecks relationships. Sin damages communion because it is the polar opposite of love. Every sin is like a spear sharpened at both ends. When you stab someone else, you pierce your own flesh, too. Every lie, every insult, every act of blasphemy and adultery scars your spirit and hardens your heart.

If a man goes to the bar with his friends after work once again and comes home intoxicated, his wife will ask where he was. "Working late," he can smirk. They both know he's lying. Worse yet, their children may witness this exchange. All members of the family go to sleep that night feeling upset and confused. The woman does not trust her husband, with good reason; their children see disrespect and dishonesty between the two people who should form the solid foundation for their lives. The communion of his family's life has been damaged by this man's one sin, and it will keep getting worse if his pattern continues. This man is living a lie. He's trying to live two different lives at once: a family man and a party animal. He is divided within himself. Which self is his true self? Which will he choose?

Our sins make us shallow, self-centered people over time. Turning our backs on God again and again will certainly isolate us and cut us off from the life and love that we crave. If you already feel separated from God, consider who moved first. Was it God? Or maybe you are the one who moved away in your relationship with God—step by step, sin by sin, more and more over the years. Slowly, you are drowning in a sea of meaningless thrills that can never replace true communion with the Father. If you don't repent, then small sins will definitely lead to larger sins—the same way a snowball picks up size and speed as it rolls down the hill.

I'M OKAY, YOU'RE OKAY?

Perhaps this all feels like too much. You may be saying, "C'mon, Fr. Joe. Enough on sin. Let's skip ahead to something more cheerful!" Popular culture might tell us that thinking about sin is misguided and bad for self-esteem. Hey, I'm okay, you're okay, right? But is this really true? Am I okay? Are you? Who decides? Doesn't God have something greater in store for us than being okay? We are beloved sons and daughters of the Father; Jesus calls us disciples and friends. God has made us "a chosen race, a royal priesthood, a holy nation, a people of his own" (1 Pt 2:9). "Okay" is a low bar. In fact, it's too low. Forget okay. We are made in the glorious "image and likeness" of God. He wants us to be in communion with him now and forever.

Ignatius asks us to seriously consider the pain and misery of sin. Like the prodigal son who wandered from home (see Luke 15:11–32), we need to reflect on our lives. How did he get to that terrible state? How did we get where we are? Like the prodigal son, we need to remember the stink of the pigsty. Really think about the shame and confusion that always results from your sins. Through this exercise, Christ will help us so that we don't run right back into more sin, sorrow, and isolation.

CHRIST ON THE CROSS

Ignatius ends this contemplation on sin by placing us before Jesus on the Cross. This is the result of sin: when we reject our loving God, we nail him to a cross. Ignatius asks us to stand with St. John, the youngest of the apostles (see John 19:25–27). We also stand with Mary, the Mother of Jesus. She is our mother, too. Speak to her from your heart. Express sorrow and contrition for your sins. Ask her to speak words of hope and consolation to you. Then, with her, speak to Jesus. Your Lord and God has come to you—making himself a man. "From life eternal,

he comes to temporal death, and so to die because of my sins"
(*SE*, 53). Look at Jesus. Reflect on your life and ask, "What have
I done for Christ? What am I doing for Christ? What ought I
to do for Christ? In this way, too, gazing at him in so pitiful a
state as he hangs on the cross, speak out whatever comes to your
mind" (*SE*, 53). Speak from your heart, "in the way one friend
speaks to another." Listen. What does he want to say to you?
Then, with Mary and Jesus, speak to the Father "as a servant to
one in authority—now begging a favor, now accusing oneself
of some misdeed" (*SE*, 54).

QUESTIONS AND ACTIVITIES

1. Read Genesis 3:1–13, the sin of Adam and Eve. Imagine this
   scene. Imagine the look on Adam and Eve's faces when they
   realize what they've done. Imagine the shame and sorrow
   they must have felt. Have you ever felt this way after your
   own sin? Write a short description.

2. Look over your life and see the patterns of sin that you have
   fallen into. Group these into different stages of life: main sins
   you committed in grade school, in high school, in college,
   when living on your own, in the last year, etc. Jot down a
   few key patterns of sins in these different eras of your life.

3. What is one central sin that you need to repent of and sor-
   rowfully offer to Christ? This could be a bad habit that has
   been with you for a long time—chronic lying, skipping

prayer or Mass, viewing pornography, etc. Ask the Lord to help you let go of this sin so that you can cling to him.

4. In prayer, see Jesus on the Cross. He is love incarnate. Pray in front of a crucifix for a few minutes. Imagine St. John and Mother Mary beside you. In prayer, ponder these questions and speak to the Lord: "What have I done for you, Lord? What am I doing for you? What ought I to do for you?" Be specific. Then, write answers in a few lines in your journal.

5. Now, turn these questions around. As you look at Christ on the Cross, ask him, "Lord, what have you done for me, what are you doing for me, what will you do for me?" (short answer: a lot, a lot, a lot!). Listen to Jesus. Write a few lines in your journal.

6. For Catholics, this might be a good time to go to Confession. If you are not Catholic, you may want to speak with a pastor or mentor about your sins and faults (see *SE*, 45–54, for more information).

A Visit to the Heart Doctor: Healing and Forgiveness

He laid hands on his eyes a second

time and he saw clearly.

—Mark 8:25

Since I was a kid, I've always been involved in sports. I've played soccer, basketball, hockey, football, and Ultimate Frisbee. I'm an athlete, but I'm not a great athlete. I love to play, but I'm lanky, clumsy, and a little too competitive. I've sprained ankles, broken fingers, and dislocated a shoulder. Crutches, casts, splints—I've had them all. I've visited more doctors, emergency rooms, and physical therapists than I care to count.

It's a familiar routine at this point: after a daring move on the field, I land with a crash and pain shoots through me. A coach approaches me and says, "Are you okay? You should probably see a doctor."

"I'm fine," I say, wincing, "I'll rub some dirt on it and walk it off."

"You should probably see a doctor," he repeats. But I still try to ignore the injury. This is difficult, since I am walking with a limp or unable to raise my arm. When ignoring it doesn't work, I start complaining.

"Dang it! This hurts!"

Friends smile, offer to help, and make the same suggestion. "You should go see a—"

I cut them off: "I'm not seeing a doctor! They're all quacks and they only tell you what is wrong with you."

"Mm hmm," a friend mumbles, "let me know if you want a ride."

I've tried ignoring and complaining; these tactics have not healed the injury. Now I move on to the next step: blaming.

"That other guy should've known I was going to fake left and then cut right! I was only following the coach's plan. And why didn't the grounds crew fix that hole or put up a sign or re-sod the field or . . ."

I tend to follow the same foolish routine with my sins. Maybe you do, too. I commit a sin due to my selfishness, recklessness, or stupidity. I screwed up. I feel awful; I've wounded my own heart. I try to ignore it, then I complain, and then I blame someone else. None of this does any good. Eventually, finally, I hear the voice of the Holy Spirit calling to me: "Go to the doctor." Only this is no ordinary doctor. This is Jesus, the divine heart doctor. Only he can heal our spiritual injuries. If I've hurt myself through sin, I've probably hurt another person, and I've hurt my relationship with God, too.

JESUS, THE DIVINE HEART DOCTOR

Jesus is a wise and caring healer. As with any physician, we must explain what happened and then show him the wound. He says, "Show me where it hurts." Our sins are a source of deep embarrassment and discomfort for us, and we hide them because we don't want others to know. Christ does not want to embarrass us nor shame us. He asks us to trust him completely, especially with our wounds. He wants to touch our hearts to heal us. This is challenging and humbling for many of us, yet it is also the one path to healing and peace.

In the gospels, we see Jesus as a hands-on, personal healer. A blind man calls out to him; Jesus spits on his fingers and touches the man's eyes (see Mark 8:22–25). People bring a deaf and mute man to Jesus; he touches the man's tongue and puts his fingers in his ears (see Mark 7:31–35). We might imagine that the blind man wears a mask to cover his disfigured eyes. Jesus removes the bandage; he is not afraid of ugly wounds. The deaf and mute man has been living on the margins of society for years; he is isolated and can communicate only with great difficulty. Jesus takes him aside and treats him individually. He deals with him personally, with the gentleness and strength that comes only from the Father's Son. It's important to remember that these physical disabilities are *not* sins, of course. Rather, Jesus' healing of bodily wounds in the gospels show us how he heals our spiritual wounds.

THREE TYPES OF HEALING: IMMEDIATE, ONGOING, AND STRENGTHENED FAITH

God can choose to heal us in different ways. First, he can heal us immediately, even miraculously. This is the kind of healing we all want, isn't it? Imagine a woman who has been estranged from her immediate family. After an ugly, public argument, she moves away and has not spoken to them for years. A friend's funeral brings her back to her hometown. At the wake, she sees her parents, brother, and sister. She feels a wave of grace and an invitation from God: "Don't wait. Now is the time." She speaks to her parents and siblings, with tears and hugs and apologies all around. After years of hurt, she feels reconciled and reunited with her family. This is communion. Christ can bring us this miraculous kind of healing.

The second way that Christ can heal us is an ongoing healing over a period of time. Imagine a man who struggles with drug addiction for years. After many failed attempts at reform, he comes to Christ in abject desperation. The man resolves once again to enter a treatment program. After a few weeks, he makes progress. He resolves, again, to stop using drugs. It takes serious effort and continued counseling. His recovery is not perfect, but he is clearly progressing. Christ is setting him free. The man knows that he must stay close to Christ and his mentors or he could easily fall right back into the darkness of addiction.

In a third way, the Lord may choose to strengthen our faith to persevere during a challenging situation. St. Ignatius was injured by a cannonball while he was battling against the French. He did not die, but he walked with a limp for the rest of his life. God did not fire the cannon, but God used this traumatic experience to renew his faith. Ignatius received this grace and re-centered his life on Christ. Perhaps you are dealing with an illness such as diabetes or a heart condition. You need to rely on family and health professionals. You must trust that the Lord is walking with you in your struggle. He, too, carried a cross. With him, we are not destroyed; rather we become witnesses to his faithfulness. Or perhaps you are separated from your spouse and reunion seems unlikely. The Lord Jesus can strengthen your faith during this difficult situation. You are not alone. Don't give up. The God of hope and love walks with you.

THE HEART OF JESUS

Jesus knows what it is like to have a wounded heart. His heart is wounded by our sins. In the gospels, we see the soldier's lance pierce his heart as he hangs on the Cross. Jesus is fully God and fully man. He is without sin, yet he willingly suffers the effects of sin: your sin, my sin, and the sins of the whole world. In paintings, Jesus' heart is often portrayed as crowned with thorns, on fire, and bleeding. Our sins wound him; yet his heart is not broken. His heart is broken open for us. He is not destroyed. Rather, we see his glory as love and grace pour out from his wounded heart. He shows us these wounds as proof of his love for us.

It feels good to finally be diagnosed and treated after an injury! My anxiety and frustrations quiet down; I'm in good hands. I've presented myself to my physician. I will get better if I follow the doctor's orders. Jesus knows us and loves us and comes to save us. Jesus, the Divine Heart Doctor, can make our hearts more like his. If we place our hearts in his hands, he can bless us and renew us.

As a priest I hear many confessions. But I don't just hear them—I go to Confession, too. I need it. I've had some terrific confessors in my life. These men help me to speak honestly about my faults and failings. They hear me, help me, encourage me, and offer me forgiveness in the Lord. They are a living example of Christ's loving mercy for me. I live in community with other Jesuits; sometimes my confessor lives in the room next to me. Sometimes I feel awkward when I knock on his door and ask, "Hey, Jim, can you hear my confession before dinner tonight?" But I'm always glad I did. In Confession, Jesus speaks words of love to my heart. He forgives me through the priest. After Confession, I feel refreshed and renewed. One Bible passage that I always think of in Confession is the parable of the prodigal son. Let's look at this passage from Luke's gospel (15:11–32).

THE FATHER'S YOUNGER SON

I've prayed with this passage many times. Through this parable, again and again, Jesus draws me into the very heart of his compassion for me and for us, as wounded sinners. Jesus speaks of a young man who asks his father for the inheritance. The son travels to a "distant country where he squandered his inheritance on a life of dissipation." Broke and hungry, he hires himself out to a pig farmer—and is still unable to make ends meet. Coming to his senses and realizing his sinful folly, he decides to return to his father's house. He prepares a speech: "Father, I have sinned against heaven and against you. I no longer deserve to be called your son; treat me as you would treat one of your hired workers." Then the son "got up and went back to his father.

"While he was still a long way off, his father caught sight of him, and was filled with compassion. He ran to his son, embraced him and kissed him . . . . his father ordered his servants, 'Quickly bring the finest robe and put it on him; put a ring on his finger and sandals on his feet.'" He calls his servants to prepare a feast to celebrate his son's return.

Throughout the centuries, this parable has been one of the most beloved in the entire Bible. I've used it on numerous high school retreats, Lenten prayer services, and in my own prayer. After I go to Confession, I often feel the peace and freedom that the younger son feels. I am forgiven and reunited with my heavenly Father.

For St. Augustine, the son's clothing with the "finest robe" was an image of priestly ordination. The father blesses the son and renews his royal heritage. Instead of filthy rags, the son now wears the noble robe that marks him as part of the father's household. The ring he wears is not simple jewelry. It is marked with the father's personal emblem—perhaps an initial or a family crest. It functioned as a sort of ancient ID card or even a credit card—it allowed the son to sign the father's name on contracts and purchases. Is this wise? The son just blew his inheritance on a wild life! But the father does not hold back; the son is fully welcomed back into communion with the royal family.

THE OLDER SON

What about the older son? He hears the music from the feast and remains in the fields. He is angry and alone. The father comes out to meet him and pleads with him. He responds to his father's compassion with anger and disrespect. "Look, all these years I served you and not once did I disobey your orders." The older son is dressed in his work clothes. He sees his father as a business manager—and a poor one, at that. Did the old man make a huge mistake by welcoming back a failed employee? Who do you resemble? The younger son or the older son?

Think about this: you are now finishing a book on Christian spirituality. My guess is that you are probably more like the older son than the younger son. Many of us feel like the younger son when we are young or in the early stages of Christian life. We often feel foolish, confused, and lost. Thankfully, someone reached out to us to guide us in our spiritual journey. Perhaps it was a teacher, a friend, a pastor, or a parent. As we get our lives under control, we become more like the older son. The older son is not all bad! The father compliments him: "My son, you are here with me always." The Father sees our faithfulness. We are the ones who show up at Mass on Sunday mornings, help with the canned food drive, and drive the youth group to the ball game. "You are here with me always." We've stayed faithful to God when so many others have wandered away. In fact, we represent the Father to the world around us. The older son is the direct heir of the father. His personality is a direct reflection of the father to the outside world. And what do they see? A bitter, self-righteous, self-centered man who cannot bear the mercy shown to his idiot brother. What will people say? "Wow, that family is really messed up. Look at the kids. You know it all starts with the parents—especially the father." How do we reflect our Father's life to the world around us?

The older son's temptation, our temptation, is more subtle and more dangerous than the younger son's. We take God's gifts for granted. We demand that he act according to our wishes. We punish those who don't measure up. Jesus prayed, "Not my will but yours be done" (Lk 22:42). If we switch that around, the results are disastrous: not your will but *my* will be done. Nevertheless, the father in the parable is compassionate to both sons. He deals with each according to his need. "My son, you are here with me always; everything I have is yours. But now we must celebrate and rejoice, because your brother was dead and has come to live again." He commends the faithfulness of the older brother as God commends our faithfulness. We are not perfect, but we have stayed with him. And he invites us to be compassionate even as he is compassionate. The father treats both sons with mercy. God does not condemn us when we fail; he wants to restore us to communion with him and with the whole family.

The parable ends, but what happens next? The younger son is inside, enjoying the celebration. The older son is outside, mulling over his options. What will he do? The father's invitation is just that—an invitation. God does not force his love on us. The father trusted the younger son enough to allow him to make his own decisions and some mistakes—lots of big mistakes! When the boy repents, his father welcomes him back. Will the young son remain with the family or go out on another binge? What about the older son? What about us? How will we respond?

THE THIRD SON

Jesus is the third son in this parable. He tells the story, and he is the eternal Son of the Father. Jesus exemplifies all that is best in both the younger son and the older son. Jesus is meek and humble of heart. He is not afraid to humble himself before the Father. Like the younger son, he trusts the Father's wisdom and love. Jesus often associates with sinners, tax collectors, and prostitutes; he is not afraid to go out to the pigsties of the world to call people back to himself. Jesus does not sin, of course. But he is not afraid to get his hands dirty to bring redemption to humanity. In response, the Father clothes Jesus with robes of glory and honor. He places a crown of divinity on his head, rings of light on his hand, and the whole world under his feet.

Jesus is also the faithful older son who dwells in the Father's house forever. Jesus keeps the Jewish customs and commandments. He does not sin, nor does he fall into a bitter righteousness. The Father commends him to us, "My Son, you are here with me always. Everything I have is yours." Jesus is the true and lasting image of the Father. Through him, the Father desires to share honor and glory with us: "Everything I have is yours." Jesus is the Alpha and Omega, the first and the last. He is the eternal, glorious, only-begotten Son of the Father; and by the power of the Holy Spirit, he is the humble son of Mary. Born in a manger, living in poverty, he is the eternal sacrament of redemption for the human race. "Come to me, all you who are weary," he says to us (Mt 11:28). "Come into my Father's house. Come back. Don't leave. You are part of our heavenly household, our loving family, and our divine inheritance. Everything I have is yours. Now we must celebrate and rejoice!"

QUESTIONS AND ACTIVITIES

1. Read Luke 15:11–32, the parable of the prodigal son. Ask Jesus, "Are my sins more like those of the younger son or the older son? How do my sins keep me away from my Father?" Answer these questions in a few lines in your journal.

2. When the younger son returns, how would he feel when he is embraced by the father? How would the older son feel

when he hears the father say, "You are here with me always. Everything I have is yours"? Recall how you felt when you forgave someone. Describe this in your journal in a few words.

3. Recall how you felt when you were forgiven by someone. Describe this in your journal in a few words.

4. Are there any people you need to apologize to? Family members, friends or coworkers? If so, now might be a good time to speak with them. If a person is deceased, you can ask Christ to deliver your apology to him or her. You may want to write out a brief apology in your journal to help you.

5. Is there anyone you need to forgive? Perhaps they have apologized to you, or perhaps not. In any case, you can pray to let go of this wound and entrust it to the Lord. If they are deceased, you may choose to write out a few words. You can then ask Christ to speak your words to him or her on your behalf and tell them of your forgiveness and love.

6. Where does your heart still hurt? Where do you still need healing? Perhaps it is in some area of ongoing sin. Perhaps you need healing from some deep hurt or resentment from your past. In prayer, invite Jesus to touch this wound in your heart; ask him to heal your wound.

EXERCISE 10

The King of Hearts: On a Mission with Christ

Take courage. It is I. Be not afraid.

—Matthew 14:27

It was 3 a.m. on a dark and windy January morning. I was sick and tired, laying half-asleep on a cold cement floor. I waited with several buddies in an underground dressing room in the St. Louis Rams' domed football stadium. I wore Mass vestments. I had my coat over my face to block out the buzzing fluorescent lights. The year was 1999. Later that morning, Pope St. John Paul II presided at Mass for more than 100,000 people in that domed stadium. I was a server at the Mass.

I was in the early stages of seminary, discerning a call to the priesthood. Weeks earlier, the seminary superior had gathered all of the St. Louis seminarians together. Each of us wrote his name on a slip of paper and put it in a giant fishbowl. The superior put on a blindfold and then drew out names one by one. "Chris Martin, Joe Post, Joe Laramie . . ." I was to be a candle bearer.

Due to security protocols, the servers had to arrive at the stadium before 3 a.m. We waited in the cold cement room for several hours before the Mass. I was getting over the flu, and I hadn't slept well the last few nights. I was nervous and excited. John Paul II had been a hero of mine for many years. I had seen him in Paris in 1997 at World Youth Day when I was just beginning my journey as a seminarian. I had read several of his books and encyclicals. I knew that he was an athlete as well as a writer, two interests I shared. He had skied and played soccer and ice hockey in his native Poland. He had led friends on hikes in the Alps as a bishop and as pope. He had been an aspiring actor before he entered the seminary. So had I. And his commitment to the faith was inspiring: he had studied in a secret, underground seminary after the Nazis invaded Poland. Following World War II, John Paul II, Fr. Karol Wojtyla, helped the Polish people to deepen their Catholic faith even as Russian communists occupied their homeland.

We were told that the pope wanted to meet with the servers before the Mass. This wasn't always possible, due to his schedule and security issues. In our weary half-consciousness, my buddies and I wondered if we would actually get to meet him. What would I say? What would he say?

I was considering a call to the priesthood. Sometimes I felt peaceful and confident as I prayed about this. At other times I

felt confused and out of place. Is that where God was truly leading me? I was good friends with several guys in the seminary.
We talked about these questions over coffee or beer. I was eager
to speak to my spiritual hero face-to-face. In this conversation,
maybe the Lord would show me the path he had marked out for
me. As it turns out, the pope did speak with me that day, and I
will remember those words for the rest of my life.

John Paul II would live only a few more years. By 1999, he
was afflicted with advanced Parkinson's disease. His hands trem-
bled slightly. His posture was bent. He had carried the Church
and the world on his shoulders for decades; he had visited every
corner of the earth. He led his people in prayer during times of
natural disaster, war, fear, and doubt. "Be not afraid!" he thun-
dered at hundreds of youth rallies, prayer vigils, and reconciliation services. "Christ yesterday, today, forever!" This was the
motto he gave to the Great Jubilee of 2000—celebrating two
millennia of the Incarnation of the Son of God. The pain and
suffering of a lifetime was evident on his face that day. Yet the
fire of faith sparkled in his eyes. His face radiated love for me, for
the thousands gathered at Mass, and the millions who watched
on TV or prayed in their homes.

As I approached him, I bowed slightly. I then looked up
and gazed into his eyes for a moment. He gazed back at me. My
nervous energy faded away. I forgot about my clogged sinuses,
my tiredness, and the fever that I'd had the day before. I felt
peaceful and safe in his presence. He opened his mouth and
said quietly, "Body of Christ."

I said, "Amen." I received Communion and went back to my seat. He had said all that he needed to say. He had shown me Jesus. This is what saints do. My spiritual hero brought Jesus to me. I said *yes*, amen! I received this gift, Jesus himself, the Eucharist—not a thing but a Person, fully man and fully God. Through his prayers at the altar, John Paul II had asked the Holy Spirit to transform bread and wine into the Body and Blood of Christ. I felt a call to do the same; to bring Jesus to others, in prayer, in preaching, and in the Eucharist.

We hadn't said much, but we'd said it all. We had said all we needed to say:

"Jesus."

"Yes."

THE CALL OF THE KING

St. Ignatius concludes the first section of the *Spiritual Exercises* with the call of the King. In this contemplation, he asks us to "place before [our minds] a human king, chosen by God our Lord himself, whom all Christian princes and all Christians reverence and obey" (*SE*, 92). He continues, "I will consider what good subjects ought to respond to a king so generous and kind" (*SE*, 94).

The desire to be part of something greater than ourselves is a very human instinct. We are drawn to great leaders who can inspire us, guide us, and bring us into community with other like-minded individuals. Together, we can accomplish far more than we could ever achieve on our own. History is filled with heroic leaders who stirred the hearts of their followers. Think of Martin Luther King Jr., St. Teresa of Calcutta, Abraham Lincoln, Dorothy Day, or Pope Francis. Pope John Paul II, now a saint, is a leader who stirred my heart.

Who inspires you? Whose vision stirs your heart? You may think of one of the heroic leaders named above. You may even consider someone who was not so famous—someone who impacted you in a personal way: a grandparent, coach, youth minister, or choir director.

JESUS CHRIST, THE KING OF HEARTS

Ignatius helps us to ponder the great leaders who inspire us. Then he points us to the real heart of this exercise: the call of Christ the King. "Gaze upon Christ our Lord, eternal King, and all the world assembled before him. He calls to them all and to each person in particular"; then Jesus says, "Whoever wishes to come with me must labor with me, so that through following me in the pain he or she may follow me also in the glory" (*SE*, 95). Jesus called Peter on the seashore one morning: "Do not be afraid! Come and follow me and I will make you fishers of men" (see Luke 5:1–10 and John 1:35–43). The risen Jesus appears to Mary Magdalene in the morning; he tells her, "Go and tell my brothers, 'I am going to my Father and your Father, to my God and your God'" (Jn 20:17).

Peter and Mary Magdalene are imperfect people, as the gospels vividly show. Peter's response to Jesus' call is, "Depart from me, Lord, for I am a sinful man." He consistently misunderstands

Jesus' teachings. He denies Jesus three times and abandons him during his persecution and suffering. Mary Magdalene is the woman out of whom Jesus sent seven demons. She presumed that Jesus' dead body was stolen; she simply wanted to weep at his grave—until the risen Jesus speaks to her one word: "Mary." Both Peter and Mary Magdalene are unlikely disciples. So are we.

You might sometimes wonder, "Does Jesus really want me as a disciple?" Our God has a habit of calling imperfect, ordinary people and doing extraordinary things with them. Dorothy Day was a single mom, an atheist, a communist, and a lifelong smoker; Christ called her into faith and allowed her to serve thousands of poor people. Moses had a speech impediment; God chose him to lead the Israelites out of Egypt and guide them toward the Promised Land. Abraham and Sarah were too old to bear a child; then came Isaac. Through this child, their descendants became as numerous as the stars in the sky. So often, our God does not call the powerful; he empowers the ones he calls. He can feed five thousand from a few loaves and fish. He can bless others through our modest gifts, if we only say yes.

"Come and follow me," Jesus calls to Peter. This is the call of Jesus throughout two thousand years. In the gospels, we see that his followers are normal, everyday folks. Young and old, rich and poor, men and women. Maybe we resist Jesus' call, like Peter, saying, "Depart from me, Lord, for I am sinful" (Lk 5:8). Jesus already knows we are sinners and that we cannot accomplish our mission alone. He calls us to work with him for the salvation of the whole world. Through us, Jesus reaches out to touch other hearts—one person at a time. He does not call the perfect; he perfects the called. We may want it the other way around: "Lord, make my life peaceful, successful, joyful—and then I'll follow you." Usually it doesn't work that way. Peter and the first disciples dropped everything they owned to follow Christ. Jesus blessed them with a tremendous catch of fish; then "they brought their boats to the shore, they left everything and followed him" (Lk 5:11).

Jesus is not a king who dictates from an ivory tower. He is Emmanuel, "God with us." He comes to us. He is the king who gets his hands dirty in the work of salvation. He is the Good Shepherd who goes out to rescue the lost sheep. He is the eternal fireman, racing into a burning building to save the trapped and wounded. He gets into the boat with us, reaches out to the leper, blesses the children, and speaks to our hearts. He works through us, with us, and in us. This is the young laborer from Nazareth; he uses his own hands to build his Father's Kingdom.

Ignatius encourages us: "Those who desire to show greater devotion and to distinguish themselves in total service to their eternal King and universal Lord, will not only offer their persons for the labor, but will go further still. They will work against their human sensitivities and against their carnal and worldly love" (*SE*, 97).

Christ calls sinners. And he raises us up from our sins. It's hard work and we must cooperate. "Take up your cross and follow me." He calls us to a life of generosity, holiness, and love. Jesus calls you.

"Who, me? You want me?" you ask.

"Yes, you. I want you," he replies. Give him everything. Don't hold back.

Christ has heroic plans for each of us. The world needs missionaries, teachers, servants of the poor; priests and deacons, religious sisters, leaders and healers. Christ may ask us to do something heroic in a faraway place. Or he may place us as shepherds and shepherdesses in our own churches and homes. Families need parents, grandparents, godparents, aunts, and uncles. Churches need someone to visit the elderly, prepare meals for the sick, and pray for those in need. Who will mow the grass for the disabled man on your street? Is there a young mom on your block who would appreciate one hour of babysitting this week? As an old poster promoting Jesuit missions read, "Some give by going; some go by giving." Christ calls some to be missionaries; Christ calls others to support those missionaries with letters, prayers, and gifts. Christ has a heroic mission for each of us. Maybe yours is in a faraway country. Maybe it's in your own kitchen or neighborhood.

I see the tender love of my grandfather, walking beside me in that rural Eden. I see the fire in the eyes of St. John Paul II as he cries out again and again, "Be not afraid." I see the young Ignatius, lying in bed, pondering his life as he recovers from an injury on the battlefield. I see the Jesuit seminarians and young priests who taught me and walked with me in high school and college. I see Christ the King speaking to me through all of them.

OFFERING OUR HEARTS
TO CHRIST THE KING

In prayer, St. Ignatius asks us to imagine ourselves before Christ the King, Mary his Mother, and the angels and saints. Take a deep breath. Put your hand on your heart. Feel it beat: *pum bum, pum bum.* Jesus made you and your heart; he now fills you with love and generosity. Again recall all that the Lord has done for you: he is so generous. Will you respond with generosity?

I'm not perfect. And Jesus calls the imperfect. This includes St. Ignatius, St. Peter, St. Mary Magdalene, and me. Jesus gives me many gifts. But ultimately, Jesus offers me himself. In return, I offer him myself. Allowing the Holy Spirit to stir my heart, I come before the Lord. I pray: "Eternal Lord, I make my offering with your favor and help. I make it in the presence of your infinite Goodness. . . . I wish and desire, and it is my deliberate decision, provided only that it is for your greater service and praise, to imitate you . . . if your Most Holy Majesty desires to choose and receive me into such a life" (*SE*, 98). I pray, simply and honestly, Ignatius's great prayer: "Take, Lord, receive all my liberty, my memory, understanding, my entire will" (*SE*, 234). I offer you everything, Lord. I offer you myself.

I want to imitate you, Lord. I accept the suffering that may come my way. I am indifferent to wealth or poverty, a long or short life. I want to labor with you, to be with you. I know that you are with me, Lord, in my moments of joy and sorrow. So, too, I want to be by your side, no matter what. Whether I experience hunger or rejection, glory and power, humility or peace. You are the principle that guides my life. You are the foundation on which you build my life—according to your designs, today and tomorrow and forever.

QUESTIONS AND ACTIVITIES

1. Read the calling of Peter in Luke 5 or the Annunciation to Mary in Luke 1. Imagine the event. What were the sights, sounds, and smells in this scene? What did Peter or Mary say? How did they feel? In your journal, describe this scene in a few words.

2. Put your hand on your heart. Recall that God made your heart, and he sees that it is "very good." Keep your hand there for thirty beats. How are you feeling right now? Write down a brief description; include physical and emotional words, such as happy, tired, and sad. Tell Jesus about this: "Lord, right now I feel . . ." Then listen. Is there anything the Lord wants to say to you?

3. Put your hand on your heart again. See Christ the King looking at you with love, surrounded by the angels and saints. With great generosity and hope, offer your heart and your life to Jesus. You might use the words from Ignatius on the page above (*SE*, 98) or the Suscipe prayer (see appendix)

to help you. How do you feel as you do this? How does Jesus respond?

4. With great generosity and hope, ask the Lord, "What do you want me to do for you?" Do you feel that God is calling you to do something special right now? Is there anything specific that you feel drawn to: Praying with your family more often? Helping an elderly person in your neighborhood? Going to Mass each Friday?

5. More broadly, how is the Lord calling you to live? For example:

   a. If you are a young person, is the Lord calling you to religious life or to marriage (and to whom)? Ask him in prayer. Be generous to him. God might answer this very clearly. Or he may point you to the next step of your spiritual journey.

   b. If you are already living your vocation, is God asking you to make a big change: maybe a new job or a new city? Or perhaps the Lord is calling you to live out your vocation with deeper purpose and devotion: to love your family more fully, to work more thoughtfully, and to follow Christ more closely. What is one specific action the Lord is calling you to?

   c. Maybe you don't fit into either of these two categories. Perhaps you feel that you don't fit into the world or the Church. Recall that God often calls unexpected people to holy missions. Remember, God has prepared a special mission just for you. Ask, "Lord, draw me to your heart and send me in your Spirit. Who can you bless through me?"

Final Heart Check

Take time to review your whole retreat. By reviewing, the Holy Spirit deepens and strengthens the graces you received. Read through the questions below. Then take some time for prayer, and jot down a few final notes. You could do this now, tomorrow, or over several days next week.

1. How was your retreat? Did you stay faithful to daily prayer and journaling? Did the retreat go as you expected? Were there any surprises?

2. Look over the notes you wrote in your journal during this retreat. What are some of the highlights and graces you received from the Lord during these days? You may want to summarize your notes on a single page. Then thank him. Savor these gifts.

3. Is there one section that you'd like to go back to—perhaps a scripture passage, a question, or a conversation with Jesus? Take some time to pray with this section again. Ask the Lord to renew and deepen this grace in your heart. Savor!

4. How did the Lord shape your heart during these days? Were there any themes or patterns in your prayer? (God's love, gratitude, etc.)

5. What grace did you ask for at the beginning of this retreat? Maybe you asked for peace, guidance, or healing. Did you receive this grace? Did God give you something different? Talk with him about this.

6. Are there any changes you want to make as you return to your daily life (watching less TV, taking more time for daily prayer, etc.)?

7. What is one practice from this retreat that you want to continue in the days ahead? The Examen? Daily journaling? A favorite prayer? Pick one or two exercises and continue doing them for the next week.

8. Is there one exercise from this retreat that you want to share with someone in your life? For example, you might show your spouse your version of the P&F. Or pray a short form of the Examen with your grandkids before dinner next Sunday. Talk with one or two friends about some of your spiritual gifts and virtues; invite them to reflect on their own gifts and talents.

9. Conclude with one more friendly conversation with the Lord. Speak with him about your retreat. Listen. Thank him.

CONCLUSION
Are We Done?

I am the Alpha and the Omega,

the beginning and the end.

—Revelation 21:6

Congratulations! You've completed your retreat! You now join the millions of Christians throughout history who have made a retreat with the *Spiritual Exercises* of St. Ignatius. Maybe you did it over ten days, two weeks, or two months. How do you feel? Refreshed? Tired? A good retreat takes work—that's why they're called *Exercises*! God supplies the grace, but we have to cooperate. With his help, we put in the time and effort for reflection, daily prayer, and personal examination.

Take time to consider what was your favorite part. What worked well for you? What worked the best? Whatever worked best, go back to it and keep working it!

Let's review where we've been. We spent time in gratitude for the gift of life and God's action in our lives. Through the Examen, we sought to grow in our awareness of God's goodness to us each day. We've reflected on the specific gifts and blessings God has given to us: our spiritual Top 10, talents and virtues, desires and interests. We are also aware of our limitations and weaknesses. We humbly turned to Christ, the Divine Heart Doctor, for healing and forgiveness.

With the two sinful sons, see that our Father's house is our ultimate source and destination. Jesus, the Eternal Son, models for us the courage and compassion that we are all called to live. We've heard Christ the King calling to our hearts. He wants us to follow him today, tomorrow, and forever. How will we respond?

You might wonder, "Are we really done?" Yes, our retreat is over. But our relationship with Christ continues. During this retreat, maybe you've set aside an hour or more each day for reading and prayer. For many people, it would be difficult to keep up that commitment for another month. Yet a good retreat should spill over into your daily life in the weeks ahead. Perhaps the Lord gave you the grace that you asked for. Perhaps you received the peace that you were seeking. Or you found a renewed sense of direction in life. Maybe you experienced real spiritual healing. Or you are prayerfully considering some significant changes: cutting back on TV, making more time for daily prayer, and so on.

What do you want to carry forward from this retreat? Which graces? Which good habits? For example, I recommend that you keep writing in your journal. Look back at it periodically—maybe once a week or once a month. Your journal can help you to revisit, repeat, and savor the best parts of your retreat. Often, the Holy Spirit deepens and confirms the graces we have received when we go back a second or third time. Ignatius recommends that we take time to repeat certain parts of these exercises. Repetition helps us to go deeper and to savor the graces. We've used many different scripture passages during these days: Genesis 1–3, the parable of prodigal son, and the call of Peter, among others. Go back to these again. Look them up. Read through them. Pray with them. Speak to Christ. Listen to him.

Ignatius has given you some new tools for your "spiritual toolbox," such as the Examen and P&F. Work these into your daily spiritual routine. Pray the Examen. Offer your heart to Christ the King. I try to keep a journal and do the Examen each day. Periodically I look through my journal and ask, "Lord, how have you been at work in my life this month?" Revisit these exercises; let the Lord strengthen your relationship with him.

Jesuits make an eight-day silent retreat every year, typically in the summer. On that retreat, I have revisited many of these meditations year after year: gratitude, forgiveness, the call of the King, etc. As I grow in my vocation and change assignments, new graces flow from these exercises. The Holy Spirit gives me what I need from these same exercises again and again. Our relationship with Christ is a living reality; it should grow and deepen as we journey with him.

In fact, your retreat was only based on the first part of the *Spiritual Exercises*. There are actually four parts! Or as Ignatius calls them, the four "weeks" of the *Exercises*. He divides the retreat into four weeks, presuming that someone makes the retreat over a thirty-day period. We focused on the first part (or week), which examines our relationship with the Lord. Key themes here include self-reflection, gratitude for God's gifts, sorrow for sin, forgiveness, and, finally, service to Christ. The second part looks specifically at Christ's Incarnation, life, and ministry. The third centers on his Passion and Death. And the fourth part concludes with the Resurrection and life in the Holy Spirit. Throughout the four weeks of the *Exercises*, Ignatius draws upon scripture and Christian tradition as well as his own insights and spiritual experiences.

NEXT STEPS

What's next? You knew Jesus before this retreat; hopefully you now know him more and love him more. He wants to keep drawing you deeper into communion with him. If you want to continue your retreat with Ignatius into the second, third, and fourth weeks, you might use Luke's gospel. Luke walks us through the angel's Annunciation to Mary, the birth of Jesus, his life and ministry, his Passion, Death, and Resurrection. Slowly and prayerfully read through Luke's gospel in the days and weeks ahead. You might take a chapter per day, or even a chapter each week. In addition, I've listed some books, websites, and resources in the appendix. These might be helpful for your ongoing prayer and study. If you're still hungry for more, look for my three bonus exercises available on my book's page at avemariapress.com.

What's a good spiritual routine for busy people today? I've been asked that question many times by students, high school teachers, and people on retreat. In a nutshell, I'd recommend these four things:

1. Take twenty to thirty minutes each day for quiet prayer, the Examen, and journaling.

2. Attend Sunday Mass each week, preferably with family or friends.

3. Go to Confession at least two to three times each year. You could go during Advent, Lent, and in the summer.

4. Make a retreat once per year. This could be over a weekend, or even one day if you are busy. Or you could use a "retreat book" similar to this one. See the appendix for suggested books and retreat houses.

Of course, you are free to mix in whatever is helpful for you. This may include the Rosary, eucharistic adoration, reading scripture (especially Sunday Mass readings), attending talks or Bible studies at your church, or reading other spiritual books (reading even a few pages a day can help; see the appendix for recommendations). You could do any of these activities on a weekly or monthly basis. Be sure that your spiritual routine fits with your vocation in life. If you are retired, you may have time to participate in several additional spiritual events. But if you're a mom with young kids, you probably don't have a lot of spare time. The Lord understands. He is with you.

Stay close to the Lord. Speak from your heart. Listen to him. Use these exercises. Review your notes. Thank him. Savor the graces. Look at Jesus. See his Sacred Heart, beating with love for you. Offer him your heart, with all of your wounds and imperfections. He is our Lord, King, and friend—"yesterday, today, and forever" (Heb 13:8)!

Prayers and Resources

MORNING OFFERING

(A prayer centered on the Sacred Heart of Jesus)

O Jesus, through the Immaculate Heart of
Mary,
I offer you my prayers, works, joys, and sufferings of this day
for all the intentions of your Sacred Heart,
in union with the Holy Sacrifice of the Mass
throughout the world,
for the salvation of souls, the reparation of sins,
the reunion of all Christians
and in particular for the intentions of the Holy
Father this month. Amen.

ANIMA CHRISTI

(A favorite prayer of St. Ignatius)

Soul of Christ, sanctify me.
Body of Christ, save me.
Blood of Christ, inebriate me.
Water from Christ's side, wash me.
Passion of Christ, strengthen me.
O good Jesus, hear me.
Within Thy wounds hide me.
Permit me not to be separated from Thee.
From the wicked foe defend me.
In the hour of my death call me
And bid me come to Thee,
That with Thy angels and saints
I may praise Thee
Forever and ever. Amen.

SUSCIPE PRAYER

("Suscipe" in Latin means "to receive"; it is pronounced:
SOO-shə-pay.)

Take, Lord, and receive all my liberty,
my memory, my understanding,
and my entire will,
All I have and call my own.
You have given all to me.
To you, Lord, I return it.
Everything is yours; do with it what you will.

Give me only your love and your grace,
that is enough for me.
—St. Ignatius Loyola, S.J. (*SE*, 234)

PRAYER OF ST. FRANCIS XAVIER, S.J.

My God, I love thee;
not because I hope for heaven thereby,
nor yet because who love thee not are lost
        eternally.
Thou, O my Jesus,
thou didst me upon the cross embrace;
for me didst bear the nails and spear,
and manifold disgrace.
And griefs and torments numberless and sweat
        of agony;
even death itself,
and all for one Who was thine enemy.
Then why, O blessed Jesus Christ
should I not love thee well?
not for the hope of winning heaven,
or of escaping hell.
not with the hope of gaining anything,
nor seeking a reward,
but as thyself has loved me,
O ever-loving Lord!
Even so I love thee, and will love
and in thy praise will sing,
solely because thou art my God,
and my eternal king.

SPIRITUAL RESOURCES: RETREAT HOUSES

There are dozens of Jesuit retreat houses in the United States and Canada. You can find a list online at jesuits.org/retreat-centers. They offer retreats based on the *Exercises* in various formats: weekend retreats, preached retreats, eight-day retreats, and so on. Most major cities have a Catholic or Christian retreat center; many offer wonderful opportunities for prayer and reflection. You can explore options in your own community using the internet or phone book.

SPIRITUAL DIRECTION

Spiritual direction is an ancient Christian practice. St. Ignatius himself had spiritual directors; he also directed others and recommended spiritual direction for retreatants. What is it? Spiritual direction involves speaking about your prayer and spiritual life with someone who has training and experience in theology and pastoral counseling. Many pastors, religious brothers and sisters, and some lay people have studied to be spiritual directors. Talking about your prayer with a director can help you to stay on track as you walk with Jesus, and they can help you to deepen your prayer and to understand how God is working in your life. Talking about your prayer with others in a small group can be another version of spiritual direction. This could be a Bible study group, your church's men's club, or another organization. Together, you all seek to grow in relationship with Christ. You trust and rely on the wisdom of the

Holy Spirit at work in this small community to guide and direct each of you. Again, it is often helpful to have one person in the group who has some sort of training in spirituality—perhaps a theology teacher, a deacon, or a religious sister. Contact your parish, church, or a retreat house for more info.

FURTHER READING

If you liked this book, here are additional books by Ave Maria Press that might be helpful for your ongoing spiritual growth:

- John Burns, *Lift Up Your Heart: A 10-Day Personal Retreat with St. Francis de Sales*, 2017. A young priest guides you on a ten-day retreat with a great saint.

- James Kubicki, S.J., *A Heart on Fire: Rediscovering Devotion to the Sacred Heart of Jesus*, 2012. Using the *Spiritual Exercises* and Ignatian sources, Fr. Kubicki leads you to a deeper encounter with the Sacred Heart. I use the image of the heart in many parts of this book.

- Christopher Collins, S.J., *Three Moments of the Day: Praying with the Heart of Jesus*, 2014. The three moments are: the Morning Offering, the Eucharist, and the Examen. Fr. Collins has crafted a compelling book based on St. Ignatius and Jesuit writings. He draws upon his experiences in classrooms, in parishes, and with families.

BOOKS BY OTHER RELIGIOUS
PUBLISHERS

- *Catechism of the Catholic Church*, 2nd ed. (Washington, DC: United States Catholic Conference, 2000). Have you ever wondered, "What does the Catholic Church teach about ___?" Find the info here in thoughtful, bite-sized pieces. I relied on this source for the exercises on gifts/vices. The *Catechism* is also available online at www.vatican.va/archive/ENG0015/_INDEX.HTM.

- Ignatius of Loyola, *A Pilgrim's Testament: The Memoirs of Saint Ignatius of Loyola* (St. Louis: Institute of Jesuit Sources, 2006). Shortly before his death, Ignatius dictated the story of his early life and conversion to a young Jesuit scribe; this is the transcript. I relied on this source for background on the saint's life, prayer, and ministry.

- James Broderick, S.J., *The Origin of the Jesuits* (Chicago: Loyola Press, 1997). Originally published in 1940, this classic has been reprinted many times. Employing extensive research and a fine British wit, Fr. Broderick tells the story of the life of St. Ignatius and the early years of the Jesuit order.

- Mark Thibodeaux, S.J., *God's Voice Within: The Ignatian Way to Discover God's Will* (Chicago: Loyola Press, 2010). This readable guide helps you discern important decisions.

- ———, *Armchair Mystic: Easing into Contemplative Prayer* (Chicago: Loyola Press, 2001). Fr. Thibodeaux teaches you how to pray better using the contemplative methods of St. Ignatius. I briefly describe contemplative prayer in the bonus exercises available at www.avemariapress.com.

- David Fleming, S.J., *What Is Ignatian Spirituality?* (Chicago: Loyola Press, 2008). This is a short, readable overview of Ignatian-style prayer. Fr. Fleming died in 2011. He was one of the giants in American Jesuit spirituality over the last forty years.

All of the authors above have written additional excellent articles and books on spiritual topics from an Ignatian perspective: on prayer, contemplation, discernment, and the Examen. Find any of them in your favorite bookstore or library or online. Here are a few more: Fr. Joseph Tetlow, S.J.; Fr. David Meconi, S.J.; and Fr. Timothy Gallagher, O.M.V.

WEBSITES

- usccb.org: This site offers the full text of the NABRE translation of scripture, daily readings for Mass, reflections, podcasts, and lots more.

- jesuits.org: Here you can learn more about USA Jesuits—our lives, our spirituality, and our ministries.

- ignatianspirituality.com: Sponsored by Loyola Press, this site offers many short articles and videos on Ignatian prayer.

- popesprayerusa.net: This is the official site for the Sacred Heart devotion, which I referenced several times in this book. The site provides resources and reflections based on the pope's monthly prayer intentions, Jesuit and Ignatian spirituality resources, and so on.

APPS FOR YOUR PHONE OR TABLET

- Laudate: It is known as the number 1 Catholic app. Laudate has the whole Bible, Mass readings, Confession guide, saint of the day, Rosary, and more. Free.

- Reimagining the Examen: This app is based on the book of the same name, written by Fr. Mark Thibodeaux, S.J. Do you want to pray the Examen but need some help? Fr. Thibodeaux guides you through step-by-step. Free.

Notes

1. Unless otherwise noted, all quotations are from the *Spiritual Exercises* of St. Ignatius, Fr. George Ganss, S.J., translation, named on the copyright page. The numeral "2" refers to the paragraph number, not the page number. These paragraph numbers are now used for the *Spiritual Exercises* by all translators and publishers worldwide. Thus, a reader could locate paragraph 2 in any translation and find the same basic quotation regarding "relishing things interiorly."

2. As stated on the copyright page, all scripture quotations are from the *New American Bible, revised edition*, accessed via usccb.org, 2018. This is the standard translation for the Catholic Church in the United States.

3. I put the entire quotation in the first person plural for simplicity. In the original, St. Ignatius switches between the first and third person. Brackets are my addition, for emphasis.

4. Fr. George Aschenbrenner, S.J., popularized the phrase "Examen of Consciousness." This is based on his highly regarded 1972 article, "Consciousness Examen," in the journal *Review for Religious*. Full text is available here: https://www.ignatianspirituality.com/ignatian-prayer/the-examen/consciousness-examen.

Fr. Joseph W. Laramie, S.J., is a campus minister at Saint Louis University, where he also earned his undergraduate and master's degrees in communications. He studied at Kenrick Glennon Seminary prior to joining the Jesuit novitiate. He studied graduate theology at Boston College, earning master of divinity and licentiate degrees. He was ordained a priest in 2011.

Laramie's ministry has included working with the homeless in Minnesota and Oregon, and with hospital patients in Illinois. He taught at Regis Jesuit High School in Aurora, Colorado, and Rockhust High School in Kansas City, Missouri, and also worked as a missionary to Mayan villages in Belize. In addition, Laramie served as a preacher and spiritual director at White House Jesuit Retreat in St. Louis, Missouri. Laramie's work has appeared on jesuits.org, *The Jesuit Post*, the Pope's Worldwide Prayer Network, the White House Jesuit Retreat blog, and SLU.edu. He has been a guest on Relevant Radio and EWTN radio.

joelaramiesj.com
Facebook: Joe Laramie SJ
Instagram: @joe_laramie_sj
Twitter: @JoeLaramieSJ